The Bachelor Chronicles

The Bachelor Chronicles

RON GERACI

KENSINGTON BOOKS
http://www.kensingtonbooks.com

Some of the content in this book has appeared in *Men's Health* magazine, adapted from columns or articles such as "The Dating Coach," "My Neighbor's Wife," "The Weasel's Way Out," and "A Headhunter for My Heart." <u>Mens Health</u> is a registered trademark of Rodale, Inc. For more information, please visit www.menshealth.com.

KENSINGTON BOOKS are published by

Kensington Publishing Corp.
850 Third Avenue
New York, NY 10022

All Kensington titles, imprints and distributed lines are available at special quantity discounts for bulk purchases for sales promotion, premiums, fund raising, educational or institutional use.

Special book excerpts or customized printings can also be created to fit specific needs. For details, write or phone the office of the Kensington Special Sales Manager: Kensington Publishing Corp., 850 Third Avenue, New York, NY 10022. Attn. Special Sales Department. Phone: 1-800-221-2647.

Kensington and the K logo Reg. U.S. Pat. & TM Off.

ISBN 0-7582-1329-8

First Kensington Trade Paperback Printing: July 2006
10 9 8 7 6 5 4 3 2 1

Printed in the United States of America

For
Mom and Dad
and
Denis Boyles

CONTENTS

Preface   ix

1. The Tattooed Waitress   1

2. The Odyssey of Alice and Nicole   22

3. The Old Flame   43

4. Making It   47

5. The Net Frenzy   60

6. Watching the Carnival   76

7. A Reporter Gets His Comeuppance   88

8. I See Single People   94

9. You're Him?   112

10. A Merry Road to Ruin   132

11. Humble Pleas From a Single American Man   156

12. I Fear I've Been too Hard on Allentown   172

13. The Borrowed Wife   174

14. Enter the Matchmaker   190

15. Killing the Column   214

16. Alone Again, Unnaturally   216

17. Nicole, Engaged   224

18. To the Moon, Alice   231

PREFACE

Please do not worry about your problems with dating. I assure you mine are far greater.

This book is the story of the last several years of my life, during which I had the pleasure and horror of having every dirty detail of my dating experiences put on public display while I was also trying to actually, seriously date women.

This is both a promise and a warning: I will give you the unfettered true account of one single man's dating life.

If you are a relative of mine whom I might conceivably see again, or someone who regards me as "a nice young man," I beg of you on the soul of the baby Christ to stop reading now and contact me. I have a special "friends and family" version of this book reserved just for you, free of charge.

If you are single and searching for someone, or were single, or will shortly be single again, you'll find yourself in this book. But your name has been changed. I hope.

Sincerely yours,
Ron Geraci

*"You're the hidden man inside every man I ever met,
and I hate you for that."*
— e-mail from Jessica J.
San Francisco, CA

"The women you date are so damn lucky."
— postcard from Andrea L.
Salt Lake City, UT

"You're the male Terry Bradshaw."
— e-mail from (confused) Michael W.
Long Island, NY

"If I were two-faced, would I be wearing this one?"
—Abraham Lincoln, Springfield, IL

CHAPTER ONE

The Tattooed Waitress

Life, faith, destruction.
It all begins with a naked woman.

1.

It's 1:40 A.M., in April 1999, and I'm sitting on a white sofa in a second-floor apartment behind the Lehigh Valley Mall in Allentown, Pennsylvania. *The* Allentown, of "they're tearing all the factories down" fame. The home of Dorney Park and Wild Water Kingdom and prodigal son Carson Kressley of *Queer Eye for the Straight Guy*. If you've never been to Allentown, swing by sometime. Have a drink at the Brass Rail on Hamilton Street. Have a meal at Cannon's on Ninth Street. Say hi to Charlie, the bartender.

Then I suggest that you go back to where you came from.

It's now 1:41 a.m., and I'm counting seconds on a white sofa. Mimi's sofa. In her apartment.

Date three is exceeding expectations.

You're going to do something very, very stupid. This beat in my head like a skipping CD. I drummed my fingers on my knees expectantly. *Something very, very stupid.*

Unless you screw it up.

Mimi walks out of the kitchen holding two glasses of red wine.

She's completely naked.

I watch her walk over to me. I have one eye high, one eye low, taking everything in.

"Good God."

I mutter this as an exclamation of awe and an acknowledgement of the man who bolted Mimi together. And He is a man, as sure as she is breathing. That, and He, are apparent in the details.

"Hello," Mimi growls. Her voice is gravelly. Low for a woman.

She hands me one glass. She sits next to me. Naked. She sips her wine. I take a quarter glass down in a swallow.

It is now clearly time to do something very stupid.

"Do you think I'm beautiful?" she asks, smiling.

My stomach spins up the inertia to make the irreversible lean. And I'm on her.

Forty minutes before this exact moment, while sharing a slice of Oreo Cookie cheesecake, Mimi mentioned that her best friend thought we should get sex "done and over with" by date three, since we dug each other and I would expect it.

But she wanted to "take it slow." She was just out of a relationship, you see. She wanted to be smarter this time. Upon hearing this, I gripped her hand and assumed the compassionate radio-therapist voice.

"Mimi, please don't think I'm in any rush," I said. Which naturally meant, "Mimi, give yourself permission to have sex tonight. Crazy sex. Doing things you've never done with any human being before, as a gift for me being so . . . so *different* from all the men who don't know the meaning of the word patience."

Exactly twenty minutes ago, we came inside her apartment, locked the door behind us, and began canoodling on her carpet. My screaming erection gave me the rolling ease of a garden rake. I slipped off her shirt and kissed her belly button. I had never conceived that a belly button could be so arousing to an unincarcerated man. Her's was utterly perfect. So small, diamond-shaped atop her taut tummy, with two tiny creases at north and south. Her belly button was a succulent appetizer. I felt fetishistic while venerating it with my mouth, moving downward in millimeters, cranking sensory videotape of masturbatory fodder that would be stowed for future dry spells.

Dates one and two had gone only this far. In both, she carefully unfastened her pants button, and slowly, deliberately unzipped them to the halfway-to-Heaven mark, showing exactly three teasing blonde hairs and that she didn't wear underwear. Both nights, when I pulled her zipper down another click, she put her finger upon it and whispered, "Soon."

Tonight, nine minutes ago, the zipper went down to the same line of scrimmage. I circled my fingertips on those three blonde strands, waiting, playing the part of the eager hopeful man. Mimi put my fingers on her zipper tab, and it went down just one more click.

Then she whipped off her cargo pants in a split second motion. *Whoosh.* Like a magician snapping a tablecloth out from under six china settings without causing one flute glass to teeter.

Her boldness was incredible. The shock instantly wiped clean every neuron in my brain, a sensation of total presence I've only experienced a few precious times in my life—and each came courtesy of a naked woman.

I smoothed my hand over her torso, down her thigh, not blinking for twenty seconds, my mouth open. Her shape was hypnotic, doing all that evolution had designed it to do. As Mimi was the first naked female I had seen in three months, except for marble ones in a museum in Rome—who weren't having any of me—every cell in my body was fighting to warm itself in her thighs.

I pulled my shirttails out from under my belt, began unbuttoning and lowered my lucky self upon her.

"We need wine," she said, curling herself to her pink-toe-nailed feet.

This was exactly four minutes ago.

2.

Now, we're on Mimi's white sofa. My face is nestled into her neck and my non-wine hand is caressing her breast.

"Well?" she says. "Do you think I'm beautiful?"

I give her the low chuckle-moan from deep in her neck. Which should say it all. Except it doesn't. Mimi whispers "Well?" again.

Five seconds pass. During any random instant other than

this particular one, my inner radio therapist could come up with twenty to thirty responses that would be worthy of carving on a tree, or at least beat "yes." Her question was simple but treacherous, like eighty percent of all questions women ask and a hundred percent of those they ask while naked. And I've now been silent for a lethal eight seconds. I'm desperately searching my memory for a cinematic reply.

"You're . . . incredible," I say.

I do not have a condom. I purposely did not bring condoms, because I had earlier decided that I should not have sex with Mimi. Ever. Her ex-boyfriend was a steroid-raging lunatic who called my apartment a dozen times at 4:00 A.M. after our first date a week ago, which resulted in a police report filed before our second date (a new record) and has me driving around Allentown with a golf club in my backseat. Worse, it's only a three iron I poached from the sample-product closet at work, and from the sounds of this guy I'd really need a driver to do him up right.

In considering this nagging trifle and a few other "different wavelength" issues, I concluded that Mimi and I had nothing whatsoever in common and, given that our dinner conversation sputters, we'd be history within four dates. Exploiting a woman's unrequited affections for sex beyond the Clintonian variety without offering her the faintest hope of a relationship—which Mimi made clear she wanted—was an act reserved for lower life-forms, I reasoned. Or at least reserved for guys good-looking enough to get away with it. It would amount to using her, I further reasoned. And I am not a user. *I despise and renounce users.*

And then there are Mimi's tattoos. Her arms have large,

gnarled inkings of hearts and roses. She had them put there in her teens, for God knows what reason. She was now thirty-three. They're garish, in one glance both an abomination and sexually electrifying. Her tattoos are so goddamn big that they simply *must* belong to a woman who will throw you on a mattress and nearly kill you, and that's during foreplay. Okay, she didn't have a skeleton riding a Harley or lizard demon belching fire on her biceps, which might garner more frightened looks at PTA meetings than her hearts and roses, but they still gave her the aura of a fertile warrior who is hot as hell but does not resemble the imagined mother of my children.

"They're fantastic," I say, moving my mouth down her bare shoulder, kissing the artwork on her right arm.

Finally, having sex with Mimi would obviously make my extraction from her life more difficult, more hurtful. So I have set my sensible parameters: I can take her out, drink some wine and eat some steak, take her home and get all my jollies while going to the precipice, at least for one or two more dates or, max, three. This beat watching HBO or spending another expensive night sitting in the bar she worked in, my usual haunt and the place we met. But, being a genteel person, I would not let sex occur because of all reasons stated and many others that I had not thought of yet.

"God almighty, do you have any condoms?" I gasp at Mimi, her knees under my chin. I'm furiously attempting to mentally will an indestructible Trojan to materialize between us, applied by divinity and blessed for multiple use. *God, please let me have the opportunity tomorrow to regret doing something stupid right now. I promise to regret it so frigging much I'll suffer like you've never seen.*

3.

"Come here," Mimi says, reaching through my shirt buttons and grasping my tuft of chest hair, pulling my face to hers. She gives me a long, deep kiss. "I told you, I want to take it slow," she says in my ear. "You'll know when I'm ready. You'll take me out for dinner, and I'll say, 'tonight, the dessert's on me.' That'll be our little signal."

I hear my penis laugh in maniacal madness.

"Okay," the compassionate radio therapist says, his voice cracking. He still managed to speak tenderly enough to insinuate that he hoped for an even more restrained plan but would accept her's if she thought it best. The radio therapist is lucky to be disembodied from the apoplectically turgid guy stroking Mimi's freshly razored legs, looking at her body, looking at that goddamn delicious belly button.

4.

It's over. Twenty minutes later, having cha-cha-ed on the precipice in every way technically possible, she's walking me to the door, completely naked, with her cat cradled in her arms. As I leave, she stands in the doorway and waves at me with her cat's paw, completely naked.

"Good-bye Won," she baby talks, as if the cat is bidding me adieu. "Wemember the signal."

5.

That was a close call, I breathed, driving home. *Thank God I kept my wits about me.*

6.

Mimi and I were not meant to be together. But, like a Republican spying a funded social service, I was having trouble leaving her well enough alone. After a dating dry spell of several months, having her forwardly announce her liking of me as I was leaving a bar represented a rare rejection-free opportunity to get a woman, and I'm far too humble a servant in God's kingdom to turn my nose up at that.

I didn't envision that taking her number in that strip-mall bar around 10:30 on a Tuesday night would be the first domino to clink over in a progression that would lead me to become a low-grade dating guru, a two-faced liar, and a perpetuator and victim of imploded relationship attempts that would cling to me like a prison record for the next six years—and counting.

The opportunity Mimi presented was one that the average employed, not-still-living-with-Mom single guy who is typically hard up simply cannot refuse.

It was a two-parter.

First, it dangled the incalculable gratification of possibly being able to add a live, warm woman's body to an intimate act, which can make an intimate act much better. Naturally, this desire is rooted in that hardwired, quietly aggressive evolutionary mission to impregnate this woman—and to impregnate all comely females and swollen supermarket produce and the coffee table if it looks at you the right way—all in the hopes of finally fertilizing that mofo-ing egg and bringing another like-faced soldier into the world. One who would hopefully cut me a break when it came time to decide which useless elder would take a little trip on an ice floe.

Of course, as evidenced by my sound decision to *not* have sex with Mimi, our cerebral cortexes have the sober power to bitch-slap down our rat brain's screaming urges to impregnate out of the fear of being bankrupted by the baby momma's lawyer. This complicates the wonderfully clear "screw-and-impregnate-first-ask-questions-later" prime directive that has served men well for eons, leaving us confused and bedraggled middle-class single guys who've never been to prison with a frustrating mission I call Defile-Lite. Translated, you may defile, but only lightly, which is not defiling in the proper sense but can feel close enough to make the night pleasant without the risks of full-blown defilement. You can dabble, play, simulate, dip your big toe in, then go in up to your knees, plant a flag five feet from the peak, write your initials in temporary marker, clean out the vault but leave the safety deposit boxes alone and then merrily run the hell out of there before the feds come.

Satisfying these benevolent impulses with the help of an actual living, on-site woman's body is, by far, the weaker of the two factors that made me dial up Mimi even after she told me that her freshly chopped ex had anger-control issues. Really, you can appease about 35 percent of these impulses by fantasized proxy through small talk with cafe waitresses and good porn. If you remain single too long, fantasized proxy can begin to seem like the most practical choice. Why? The other 65 percent of bliss that a warm-blooded bedmate brings can also bring stinging risks, stratospheric financial expenses, and—if word gets around and you're not particularly proud of your choice of bedmate—the potential loss of an imminent better bedmate who was about to reveal herself. Men were never meant to subject sex to a risk-vs.-benefit analysis, but I do—mostly when I'm not laying on a carpet with a completely naked woman.

The second component of the opportunity Mimi offered me was the violent stoking of a small, flickering flame of a childhood-born expectation and optimism that is critical to a single guy if he's going to refrain from hurling himself off of a twenty-story building. That flame is the faith that *it will happen*. If Mimi wanted me, it's logical to believe that another woman—the one I've been waiting to meet, who is so hot and kind and loving and so way out of my frigging league that it's absurd—could conceivably want me, too. Or at least not immediately vomit at my sight.

Having this little flame of faith stoked by a hand-licking lover is about the best reason a man will ever have to feel pompous when he walks out into the morning air.

On the flipside, that weak flame of hope comes so close to being snuffed out during months and years of rejections and "she's okay for now" dating in the twenties and thirties, it can torture a man with the cold, depressive thought that amounts to him realizing his mortality. Or realizing that his horizon is finite and his life may be just one more of the inconsequential billions laden with toil and disappointments and uncelebrated smallness. Or realizing that he'll never achieve anything but the ordinary and his big dreams were the dreams of a loser and a fool.

This cold, depressive thought is, "Maybe Alice *was* the best I'll ever do."

We'll talk more about Alice later.

7.

Mimi could stoke my fire. She was an oasis in the desert of Allentown, which is the same desert a guy on the shy side encounters everywhere he goes, from Philly to Bangkok. If I hydrated myself on her charms, I might just make it to Mecca and find that life-changing girl—without becoming a parched skeleton that best served the earth as bird food.

And Mimi had a great ass. So I called her.

8.

"So, what do you do when you're not waiting tables?" I asked her during our first call, fumbling to find something to connect us other than both being single and living in the same state.

"I'm an artist," she growled in her low, granular voice. "I weld steel into abstract sculptures."

I mentally processed this and envisioned her in a helmet, sparks flying like holy hell, her grit-speckled tattoos glistening with sweat.

"Do you do anything creative?"

"I draw," I said instantly. It shot out like a reflex. It was utterly false. I've developed a respectful awe for the animalistic, scrappy engineers who man the circuitry of my subconscious. They do nothing constructive or useful for months at a time, and just when I'm sure they're gone and have finally left me to my own peril, they press the intercom button and take over.

At this random moment they said that we draw.

We don't.

"What medium do you use?" Mimi asked.

"Charcoal," they replied.

"That's interesting. You're interesting," Mimi said. "What subjects do you usually draw?"

"Boxers," they said.

"Like who?"

"Rocky Marciano. Mostly."

There was a short pause. In this brief window, a subconcious memo was issued that explained these responses.

If she welds steel to make metal sculptures, you can't damn well tell her that your most rugged artistic outlet is editing "Male-grams." "What are they? Why, Mimi, they're short informational and entertaining news-you-can-use ditties in the front of the magazine I work for." Go ahead and tell her about the one you're working on about the benefits of chai tea. So we said drawing. Charcoal comes from sixth grade. "Boxers" was a curveball to shut her down and get to another topic. She knows as much about boxing as you know about Matisse. The follow-up question was not expected, so we pulled out Rocky Marciano. It was the first dead boxer in the file cabinet whose name sounds like a famous boxer, so she might be embarrassed about asking who it is. (Gene Tunney would not have worked for this reason.) Rocky Marciano will be arcane to her and will end this. You'll be back to

*talking about her fellow waitresses with cocaine habits in exactly
one second, and you will never discuss art again. You'll have gotten through these few seconds with masculine dignity by using an
unverifiable lie that may, we hope, leave her with the impression
that you're a deep-souled artist worthy of, at the least, fellating.
On an unrelated note we continue to be disappointed in you and
we may discuss this and other issues tonight as you try to sleep,
depending on how the rest of this conversation goes.*

"Rocky Marciano. . . ." Mimi said slowly, thinking.

"You don't mean Graziano. . . . You mean the heavyweight champ from the fifties, right?"

"That's him," I said cheerfully, wanting to blow my brains
out.

"I would love to see your drawings."

"Of course, they're right here. I'll show them to you when
you come over to my apartment."

9.

"So what did you do?" Denis Boyles asked me four days
later in the *Men's Health* offices. He was an esteemed writer, a
long-time columnist and the staff sage. He had recently
started working in the office after being tethered to the magazine remotely for a decade.

"These," I said. I showed him a piece of copier paper with
a charcoal sketch of Rocky Marciano on it. He was depicted
marching to a neutral corner after dispatching Jersey Joe
Walcott in a 1952 fight. Another leaf of stolen copier paper
showed Rocky Marciano in mid-fight, looking straight at us,

his gloves at his hips. I explained to Denis that I had bought a pictorial book of boxing history that had three photographs of Rocky Marciano, picked up some charcoal and a sketchpad at an art store, and spent two full nights creating the sketches.

I had signed and dated them in the lower right-hand corner.

"She's obviously going to ask to see them and I needed to have something," I said. "I'll pull these two out of this satchel and tell her that they're rough studies, and all the others are in boxes and I'll show her them some other time."

Denis looked at the sketches and then looked at me for a few beats.

"You have to be joking," he said.

It wasn't a perfect plan but it made perfect sense. I was going to reiterate that Mimi was easy on the eyes, except for those tattoos that added their own spice, but that was obvious since I had put in this effort.

"Why didn't you tell her you were a writer?"

"It didn't occur to . . . look, she said she welds steel to make these huge artistic sculptures. Writing just seemed kind of pansy-ass next to that, and . . . I have no idea why I told her I was a charcoal artist. But regardless, she's gonna ask to see the sketches so I needed something."

I had concocted the idea that her steel sculptures were huge, since I've never seen anyone welding a desk ornament. And thinking that she was creating room-sized monsters of all sorts made it easier to justify having laboriously made these two beautifully rendered charcoal sketches.

Denis laughed heartily.

"You *really* think these will fool her?" he asked.

"Fool her?" I retorted, insulted. "What, they're not good? Even as just rough sketches? I think they're pretty good. They took me two nights."

"They look like a five-year-old drew them," Denis said. "Ron, if these actually fool her . . . Don't show her these. Really. Don't."

I went from insulted to hurt.

"Gimme that," I said, and I put my sketches away. Mimi wouldn't see them. Nobody would see them. I spent two nights in my apartment in Allentown—not drinking—while making these drawings and to boot got charcoal all over a Hanes undershirt and was not certain it would wash out.

10.

"This has to be the most absurd dating gambit I've ever heard," Denis said, astonished.

I would not tell him about shaving my body to back up a lie that I was a semi-competitive swimmer. Or about when I hurriedly rented a new car for a date after I noticed my own car was missing a hubcap. Or about the afternoon that I feigned a convulsion on a tennis court to get assistance from a woman batting balls forty feet away. Or about when I left my number on a phone answering machine after I dialed a wrong number because the woman's voice was sexy.

The sketches were relatively trivial in my cosmos of dating gambits.

In digesting this, it would seem that anyone who would go

to these measures would have no difficulty walking up to a woman and saying, "Hi."

Quite the opposite.

Single guys who fear looking like an ass and want to protect their egos will, on regular occasion, swing manically from their usual hypervigilance to making an all-out effort to *really* protect their egos, by deciding that if they don't seize the immediate chance right in front of their face in the constant stream of wasted now-or-never opportunities, they will have proven to themselves that they're incapable of ever seizing any chance.

So we lash out and convulse on a tennis court. Or shave our nipples. It's a bit like the schoolkid who regularly gets the shit beat out of him by larger boys suddenly finding himself walking out into the school yard and heading straight for the biggest bully, rolling up his sleeves and thinking, *Not today.*

11.

I had told Mimi this artist lie for no fathomable reason that withstood the light of day, and I had to back it up. I couldn't bank on her forgetting about it, from her reaction. My integrity was at stake if she realized I made up the charcoal-sketching crap. A lie is a lie, and you can't go back on a lie.

I mentioned to Denis, roundabout, that in the running life of a single man in his thirties—specifically one who's robustly horny, lonely, drunk a few nights out of the week, just good-looking enough to impress women he does not like, and altogether too proud and full of healthy self-respect to think he deserves anything less than Her—that funny, smart, beautiful, matching-puzzle-piece girl he was guaranteed by some cosmic contract since less deserving men were getting theirs *every goddamn day* right in front of his eyes—well, this guy was all about dating gambits.

"Telling her I was a charcoal artist was stupid, but what are you gonna do?" I said philosophically, quoting my dad's response to most earthly occurrences. I thought that it nicely summed up all of the above sentiments.

Denis, having once been single—and, he revealed, having once sent a woman across the bar a grilled cheese sandwich rather than a drink—finally confessed to understanding.

"Would you write up a little box on this for the back section?" he asked. He said he could envision doing a small, ongoing dispatch in every issue of the magazine on what was going on in my quest to find a willing woman. "We'll call it 'This Dating Life,'" he said.

12.

To say I loved the idea would be a gross understatement. It had the singularly perfect quality of being about me.

The other reason I loved it was selfish.

Like most magazine editors, I went into this line of work in order to have the world verify the notion that I, indeed, was a talent of such prodigal proportions that the most megalomaniacal daydreams of my adolescence would prove to be naively humble. Magazines would simply be a quaint prologue for this giant-to-be in the world of American—nay, global—letters, a writer and wordsmith who—once the right switch was tripped and the full wattage of his fearsome genius was liberated on (1) those choice individuals with the aptitude to recognize it and the power to disseminate it and (2) the fawning populous at large—would change the landscape of literature forever. Which would also justify his never having bothered to read most of it.

Seriously, very few magazine editors come out of high school thinking, "I'm gonna be an internal auditor and then get my CPA, and aw, screw it. *Esquire*, here I come." Talk to them, and you'll find the trajectories are fairly similar.* Most were kids who grew up reading too much, sucked at math, and then, as a consequence, decided that they had a flair for words. On the introverted-misfit scale, they moved the meter more than most. Breaking yards-per-season records on the football field, and getting laid, were highly infrequent occurrences for most. They might have actually made fun of the band geeks while editing the school newspaper. Maybe they read Mark Twain or Joseph Heller and decided that all the witty comebacks they had thought of ten minutes or ten years too late, and all of the people they wanted to humiliate or stagger . . . why, it could all still happen. Just later.

Yes, all in good time.

It was then they knew they wanted to GET PUBLISHED. So they began buying books and magazines about getting published, some with titles such as *Get Published*. And they

---

*One slight deviation to this well-worn route into publishing involves law school and law-firm refugees, who become magazine editors or writers in much the same way they become anything, "please God, anything" else. They often harbored the same "I write special" visions in childhood as most others in publishing, but they usually experience their "I'm meant to be published" revelation and the rest of the process in their twenties, after they conclude that being a lawyer bites.

learned all about things such as first North American serial rights before they had published so much as a car-for-sale ad in the local shopper's guide.

Once in college, these fancies either swung to "journalism," which meant getting published the easier way, or "creative writing," which meant "If a drunk farmer like Faulkner can scribble himself into immortality, then you'd better get out of my way."

Many excel at the university. Hell, writing doesn't take a lot of technical memorizing. You don't have to "show the work." You don't have to pass classes on the thermodynamics of heat transfer or learn C++ programming. As with rap music or poetry, anybody can do it with nothing other than hubris and a ballpoint pen. And as for being good . . . why, you might be good without even knowing it. You could conceivably write something like "So much depends upon a red wheel barrow glazed with rain water beside the white chickens" by sheer chance, and get yourself in the Norton Anthology with an ominous little dash to the right of your birth date, patiently waiting for you to get cirrhosis. Few people, however, solve nonlinear algebra equations by accident while doodling on a Starbucks napkin.

Luckily, upon the first serious encounter with an editor who's actually trying to work with them rather than inspire them (which is mostly during the first week on staff at any publication), these notions are usually stomped out like a flaming bag of shit left on a doorstep on Mischief night. Being a supposed journalist (or a creative writer hoping to use a magazine as a vehicle and venue to world renown) is making fifty calls to find out who imports the most Brie cheese in

South Dakota? It's working nine days on a 950-word piece that's cut down to a phone number? It's working for people, who, at the heart of it, don't give a crap about how I think and feel and observe and poignantly express myself with brilliant touches of irony?

Yes, yes, and pretty much.

"Well *ef this*," a good many casualties say, smartly. "I'm going into PR and at least make some money."

Hence, for most magazine editors who stay magazine editors for more than a month or two, the idealistic plan of "having a platform to be discovered" typically settles into "getting this fucking piece done and hoping it won't suck so bad that I lose my job."

But the flower of egotism cannot completely die.

It even reblooms for a few moments when the joke in the third sentence in your five sentence review of a Bic razor survives into top-edited copy and you think to yourself, *Yes, the time has come.* This warm smugness is even more satisfying if it lasts a few days, which can happen if the blurb and your joke isn't killed to make room for an oatmeal recipe until the very day the magazine ships to the printer.

13.

Denis Boyles, the legendary man who wrote with such a distinct power and ease that reading his essays had first lured me into magazines in the late eighties, was now asking me to write my personal accounts and musings on my dating life. I had been at *Men's Health*, and in Allentown, for several years at this point, I was running short on wide-eyed giddiness, and

Denis had long gone from being a mythical God behind a by-line to a friend. But the weirdness of this conversation wasn't lost on my inner nineteen-year-old.

"Absolutely," I answered.
"You might end up finding a wife this way," Denis said.
"Or losing one," I replied, laughing.

CHAPTER TWO

The Odyssey of Alice and Nicole

1.

In the life of every single man there is his Kilimanjaro, the epitome of womanhood who, at some point, he resolved was the only woman on the planet who could, and could alone, make his existence on earth a tolerable one.

She goes by many names. Some decades ago she was wistfully known as "the one that got away." More recently she is less wistfully known as "that bitch."

She's the woman who, for no other reason than a man allows her, turns his once placid days and nights into a raging arena of bile and disgust, interspersed with brief periods of the most pleasant moments life can author.

Every man has his.

To not is to not have lived.

Importantly, this isn't love.

2.

Mine was—though the past tense really never applies, if the mental affliction was properly wrought—a high school girl from the next town.

Yes, original.

I once read in a book of New York City cabbie quotations, "A woman will always return to the man she loved the most, while a man will always return to the woman who loved him the most."

Unless faulty memory has reversed the actions here, it's a dead-on mark of why "the girl that got away" gets away, and why a man, in the dark night of his lonesome soul, is left to think, "Maybe Alice would take me back again."

My homegrown target of predilection, Nicole, spent years at the edges of my consciousness in which I happily thought nothing intensely romantic about her. She was sweet, and kind, a piece of my past, then the provisional "break in case of emergency" girl who I, like most guys fixing themselves up for a tour of hell, assumed I could always seek out with resigned intentions and take as my own. That would only be necessary, of course, in the very slim chance that the vast shining frontiers ahead of me didn't toss out ten mates far better than her.

3.

To understand how she could travel from such a dismissed periphery to the smoldering ground zero of my soul, you need to know a few more details that define a Nicole.

A Nicole may, at some point, be in love with you. And she might even be placative; the type of girl who will cook you dinner and darn your shirt button, and service you while menstruating, and send you cookies at work. Sometimes all in one day. But with a Nicole, a man will think at some point, for days, weeks or months, which sometimes accumulate in many random minutes over a long period, "Yes, I *could do this*. I love this girl. I *could* love this girl. I want her in my life, as my wife. *Forever*. Almost absolutely."

A Nicole slowly seeps into your brain, and she'll likely never be fully expunged. Like prune juice on a white carpet.

The film-negative opposite of Nicole is an *Alice*.

Most men have an Alice in their past or present orbit, though she often suffers the total eclipse of Nicole.

An Alice does many of the same things that a Nicole does, but with Alice, you keep arriving at a conclusion that you'll regret one day because while it was true, you could've decided to ignore it and just be a sport about the whole thing since she loved you so goddamned much. But no. Your steady thoughts are, "Oh, Christ, why are you still doing this? You're going to devastate her when you leave. Tomorrow. Or right after her birthday next month."

Why?

Alice immediately disqualifies herself from entering your inner circle of worship due to a few key factors. First, most typically, Alice might be a tad bit plain, which spurs you to think you could do better, if you had more money or took fifteen pounds off your gut. Second, she probably thinks you're utterly incredible and is like a self-esteem–challenged puppy in her deranged veneration of you, what with the public hugging and kissing and cooing and calling you every two hours. This isn't merely totally insane (knowing what you know about yourself); it means by mathematical law, someone far, *far* hotter and more perfect would at least dig you, to a small degree, and therefore be winnable with a smidge of effort. Alice takes no effort, except for the mental forbearance of tolerating her and the taxing feelings of charity you endure while allowing her to practice her religion of you.

In the law of jungle justice best summed as "Everybody plays the fool," your Alice can become your Nicole. The soil is fertile for this if you try to reestablish your unconditional dominion over her at some point down the road (once you've owned Alice, in adolescent reasoning, you mentally claim the perpetual right to always own Alice no matter what the hell she's doing or who she's married) and she shows *genuine indifference*.

This snaps about nine laws of the universe, as genuine indifference is extremely hard for an Alice to feel, much less fake, since you badly wounded her once. A violent rebuke is sad and expected; poor Alice. Consenting to be yours again is even sadder (what, did she alone satisfy the 1974 birth quota for suckers?). A cool and restrained but subtly perturbed rejection, citing how sorry she is for you, or even a tiny laugh in your face, is just a bit less expected than the maelstrom of indignant denial. There's still *love* in all of these, you see. And since you never really loved Alice, but you could really use her again right at this particular lonesome moment, knowing there's still love there . . . well, it gives that dying internal flame of faith a puff of oxygen.

Indifference?

Impossible. Intolerable. Unacceptable. It confirms the coldest, most gruesome fear any man harbors, just under those directly concerning the continued breathing of a spouse and children. This is the fear that you are truly a piece of flotsam that can be wiped from even that very particular individual consciousness on which you stamped your most indelible, burned-through-to-the-other-side influence. If Alice can ultimately jettison you like so much belly-button lint, your mother and father can forget you. Your kids can forget you. *Really* forget you.

This is all naturally worse if you married Alice.

And many guys marry their Alice. The cabbie said they would. If they're still together after their thirties and forties, when both mature, the smart man will never let her know she was his Alice. And she'll never suspect it.

It's best if Nicole stays far away from their happy little cottage, too.

4.

While I never saw it coming, any man who's been skinned alive by a Nicole could have spotted mine a decade out. She possessed the near perfect combination of large and small Frankensteined qualities that make a lethal Nicole in waiting.

First of all, Nicole was from my home area. She knew my mother and father. As you venture further from your own little shanty, gladly distancing yourself with the speed and disgust that indicates normal social development, the people who knew all the people you love—and say some words in exactly the way you wish you could stop saying them (in Philly/South Jersey, home is pronounced *hoe-mmm*)—grow rarer. This flight is a purposeful goal for the first three decades of life. Then you slowly realize that the little places everyone else escaped from were just as crappy and stifling and dull as yours, if not far worse, so it justifies feeling nostalgia and a slight rekindled sense of affection for your own launching hovel.

When you yearn to hold one more piece of hoemm, your Nicole doesn't only speak your language, she speaks it as bad as you do.

Secondly, my Nicole was charitable-minded. She changed diapers on HIV-infected kids, worked in welfare programs, and volunteered in some such and other whatchamcallits and donated to this and that, the specifics of which I might remember if I had been listening to her when she explained these entities and their societal necessity at length.

Distilled, this didn't just mean that marrying Nicole might ensure a steady supply of refrigerator calendars; it strongly suggested that she probably wouldn't toss my infant down a ravine or make me write a song like "Ruby" if I had a Christopher Reeve–type accident. Nicoles must be able to be *envisioned* as being maternally inclined, even if they actually can't work a safety pin or cook Cheerios.

Third, Nicole was very pretty. Still is.

Nicoles must be *pretty*. They cannot be wildly hot, because a Nicole must at least remotely fit into the mental screenplay of happily making toast in a row home for the rest of her life, if that's the last-resort inevitability. A Nicole who seems more fit to be escorting some middle-aged guy on a Learjet or wearing stilettos without irony is, of course, not a Nicole at all. At least to you.

Finally, it greatly helps a Nicole-in-training if she picks a string of boyfriends who you feel are categorically inferior to you in some important way. This helps generate the occasional take-her-or-leave-her regard, underpinned with your safely assumed ability to take her anytime she was done playing with idiots, which is critical to the future hell she'll put you through.

Her boyfriends can be broke alcoholics or arrogant Wall Street dicks, pot-smoking bricklayers or effeminate chefs, wiry runners majoring in engineering or wholly transparent foreign men with apartments full of photographic equipment. Frequently a Nicole will have an extreme devotion—she'll be an Alice—to a bumbling guy who treats her like an Alice. Codependence is a beautiful quality in a Nicole. It's almost requisite, because while being codependent with another guy is pathetic, a Nicole who is codependent with you . . . it conjures the vision of an Alice you could actually love back.

The only absolute must is that each and every one of Nicole's lovers—or at least the ones you hear about—are clearly inferior to you in some loosely justifiable way, even if one or two of them is a basically nice dolt you'd gladly have a beer with.

It isn't hard to make this happen.

With a cup of coffee and about nine minutes, I could reckon several ways in which Copernicus, Gandhi, and Batman are inferior to me, which is part of the self-religion a single guy uses to ensure there's a reason to wake up tomorrow.

Finding pitiful and detestable human defects in each of

Nicole's love interests (and she'll gladly tell you what they are, in detail, as you're probably her ear) lowers Nicole's mate value in your eyes just enough to keep her at the fringe of your alleged better judgment, where she is a pleasant fixture but also an annoyance in her ambiguity. You often wish she'd marry one of these smackheads so she'd go the hell away. The caliber of the men Nicole *actually desires* is a crystal-clear message from God that you'd sully yourself if you ever joined their ranks, even though you'd be doing her a grand favor by going in and sweeping her decks clear of these losers.

Which you could do tomorrow if you wanted to sully yourself.

5.

Where's the consummation?

In talking with hundreds of regretful geeks and delusioned single guys in their thirties and forties, torrid sex between a man and his Nicole only happens in about half of the cases, and it's usually a brief affair. An essential requisite of being a Nicole is elusiveness, first with your blessing and then with your rage. In the seminars I've done and e-mails I received after starting the "This Dating Life" column (more on that ridiculous phenomenon later), many men of perfectly marriageable ilk have harped about their Nicole. Many of these guys have spent years—some, more than a decade—buying their Nicoles dinners and gifts, and buying themselves time and hope.

For the roundabout one in two who shattered this stasis and actually grabbed Nicole's funbags, they initially figured she'd relent her asinine reluctance and bullshit reasons for rejecting them. When she didn't, several admitted that they sprung into a full-blown fury of spastic attacks and vengeance and heart-ripping hurt.

I'm one, as we'll soon see.

The comparative cinematic example that these saps, aging Alices, hoards of romantic wishful thinkers, and other self-appointed sages, writers and relationship pundits invariably point to is, of course, the cute little farce of a film called *When Harry Met Sally*. Or, more recently, *There's Something About Mary*, which could be entitled *There's Something About Nicole*.

The first movie leads us to believe that Meg Ryan, who plays the part of the woman, is actually Billy Crystal's Nicole, even though he doesn't know it until three-quarters through the second reel.

Plausible. She has many of the qualities of a Nicole, which is solely why Meg Ryan once enjoyed something of a career. And Billy Crystal, in a highly euphemized form that shows none of the actual horrors of ineptitude and unfitness most Nicole-pining single guys display, whines for Meg when she turns cold on him. By the happy resolution of the film, Meg has seen the light and avails herself to be 95 percent of a *genuine* Alice to Billy Crystal, if he would just keep on saying how much he loves her idiosyncratic methods of mailing letters and serving saucy desserts.

The problems here are myriad. They're being addressed in Rob Reiner's beleaguered sequel, entitled *When Sally Divorced Harry's Ass*, which is held up in studio conflicts.

First, a genuine Nicole is not a woman but a fabricated concoction of idealized qualities—even her infuriating flaws become charming idealizations—because these qualities are observed selectively and half-assedly *from afar* and never test-driven *on a five-year live-in basis*. To capture a Nicole is to kill a Nicole. Figuratively, and, at least a few times a year in the New York region, as the *Post* thanks God for, literally.

A man doesn't truly love a Nicole, he loves the idea of her. And it's this love of the idea, her imminent Nicole-ness, that keeps these guys sniffing around Nicole with halfhearted hints and conceited retreats for years and years (and, in the cases of many of the guys who attend my seminars, *years*) without hazarding to destroy the precious myth that they could have her by bringing things to a crisis point and whipping it out.

When a crisis point hits—Meg Ryan tells Billy Crystal to go to hell—a man can confuse the frustrated and severe *indignity* of the rejection (those other losers, yes, me, *no?*), and the terror of facing the death of a myth he's rested his ego as a virile man on, *for actual love*.

Sweaty palms. Butterflies. Smashed butterflies. Broken furniture and blood all over his apartment.

It feels a lot like love.

If Nicole gives in, which she will not if she has a choice, a man in Billy Crystal's place will have preserved his life-affirming myth of attaining the nonexistent and eternally hunted "Nicole-Alice," only to have it killed, suddenly or slowly, by reality. Usually as soon as Nicole shits in his bathroom.

Another disconnect is that Meg Ryan gives Billy Crystal an Alice screw in a moment of self-pity, after she gets dumped by some dude, and Crystal is weirded out by it. This can happen, and even happen in just this way. But it's far more likely for a Nicole to give a troubling and awkward pity-screw to her delusional worshipper in his time of trouble, knowing full well that she is not what he has held her to be, glad of that fact, and only hoping that this bizarre half hour passes quickly and her social circle isn't destroyed by the fallout when she tells him it was a one-shot.

The inequity of feelings and lack of requited romantic affection (not actual love, but its fragrance) between a man and his Nicole make the possibilities for a relationship fairly goddamned doomed, which any Nicole will tell you, and any relationship writer or other pundit as aforementioned will blather on about. (Every Nicole knows whose Nicole she is, and enjoys being a Nicole as long as he doesn't put her on the spot by acting on it.)

The union is doomed because it's built on fakery and conjured feelings of having settled and having been duped. Within a few years, after Ryan tires of pretending she can be Crystal's Alice, or Crystal tires of pretending Ryan is any facsimile of the Nicole he wasted so much time, hair and psychic energy on, it's over. Nicole walks out first, depending on the constraints added by children.

Happily, this eventuality is rare, as most guys are initially too smart and then long too meek to mess around with their Nicole, since many of their needs are nicely met by Alice, whom they still plan to dump next week. Nicole returns the favor by being too smart to mess around with her hallucinating masochist.

6.

Regarding my own Nicole, my first clichéd crisis point came in September 1996, when she broke her record of bedding dismissible twerps I knew or cared little about for a dalliance with a man I liked and admired.

My blood turned into lava.

I seethed with an immature indignation and jealousy that only Sicilians and career Broadway understudies might truly understand. I was ready to kill children and kittens. I stared into the black universe behind my rural garage-top apartment in Allentown at 3:30 A.M., having drunk heavily, and prayed for some higher power to take my rage and exterminate those responsible and also exterminate their friends and children and kittens for good measure.

I was bile-choking mad.

In the fleeting moments of clear thought, I ran down the top ten still-logical reasons I had considered and dismissed Nicole as girlfriend potential since I was an acne-riddled teen with frightfully lush chest hair atop my frightfully advanced gynecomastia. These reasons are typically cited in Nicole situations, as I came to learn.

1. She didn't get my jokes. Since my jokes are as deft and incredible as every guy knows his jokes to be, this should've nailed the coffin shut.

2. When I took Nicole out, it was as fun and diverting as being out with my mom, except for the occasional thrill of seeing cleavage that was in no way associated with my mom. Time with her was enjoyable, nice, looked forward to, well spent, appreciated. But the low-voltage tingling I'd expect to feel in my testicles when with someone I highly desired was more of the usual hum.

3. She dismissed our chance meeting of Roddy McDowall in a drinking lounge in a Philadelphia hotel as absolutely unremarkable, whereas I nearly wet myself. This was an important cue of incompatibility I could not readily identify.

4. If my feelings about her were actually translatable into something hot and romantic I would have acted on them a long time ago on any number of occasions.

5. Politically and societal-consciously, I was far more apathetic than she was, and this disparity would get old extremely fast unless I either started grooving on the idea of caring about other people and the state of the planet or could take long and frequent vacations from her.

6–8. I couldn't fantasize about her sexually to any productive end, despite occasional conscientious attempts. That's gotta mean something.

9–10. She dated jackasses, miscreants, boobs, pansies, derelicts, and everyone else with traits I don't associate with myself unless forced.

I deliberated the above list soberly, and weighed it against the one lone umbrella pro that encapsulated all of her Nicole

qualities: Inwardly, I strongly agreed with the survey state-
ment "I often believe I could actually love her and like it."

So I decided to do the only proper thing.

The next time she called me, I told her to screw off.

I told her: Have a great life, you're not who I thought you
were, you're what I thought you were not, you won't have
Dick Nixon to kick around any more, good luck and God
bless, this time your hurtin' won't heal, one would think I deserved better, stop telling me that he came on to you because
it's vile and *I don't care*, you've ruined my friendship with
him, you never gave a goddamn about me so why are you so
upset now, say hi and bye to your mom and dad, don't call,
we'll always have memories, as I'm wholly dismissible to you
so now I elect to be wholly dismissed, take care and all that,
bye. Now really, bye.

At some point during this farewell address, Nicole said
something insightful.

"You've always made me out to be something I'm not," she
said, half-crying, half-angry, half-wishing I was somebody
else so all these futile emotions might be worth something.
"You always put me on a pedestal."

"I wish you could see yourself the way I saw you," I replied.

In the coming years, I'd learn that the idiocy of this comment, of this wish, is the root of all vain Nicole conun-
drums.

7.

Following the typical post-climactic Nicole script, things
didn't go well after that last phone call on a September Saturday morning in 1996.

I wanted to restore the trusty, reassuring myth of having her as a final refuge more every week as fall turned into winter. I tried to replace her with a local girl who sold corporate newspaper ads, then an old college friend, then late hours at the office, then alcohol. Her absence, which was the normal status quo except now it was with prejudice, festered like a cancer in my brain. I spent many hours trying to reckon just how something that had been so benign for so long could have such a sickening impact on my day-to-day life.

"You'll get over it," my coworker, Greg, absently told me. "You shouldn't have played hurt to get what you want."

You have no conception of the intensity of my rage and how badly I want my life to be destroyed, I thought.

He didn't. Because he couldn't. The exhilarating pain of the wound that involves a man's Nicole can only be experienced in real time, not imagined or remembered.

Men who have never tasted it could never fathom the ridiculously unnecessary searing agony of being skinned alive by a feather and then feeling your bloody flesh burned by the blowtorches of routine daily events, of the absurd continuing existence of champagne and sunlight and people laughing around you. And Bryan Adams songs. And well-wishers who sense something is wrong and tell you that you'll get over it.

Men who have spent time in this quadrant of hell, on the other hand, know that you get over it. And getting over it means gaining an amnesia that's necessary for survival, an amnesia that restores the logical certainty that nothing that involves such whisper-soft forces and phantoms of thought could possibly deliver a pain of that ferocity.

At least not without killing you instantly and immolating your bones.

Not if you get over it.

Through September and October, and November and Christmas 1996, earth was a bitch. I numbed. I drank. I marveled at what nothing could do if you let it out of its cage.

Then, of course, it happened.

In March of 1997, during a particularly bad bender, I dialed the phone, figuring . . .

Christ, I have no idea what was going through my sick head. Perhaps I was figuring I would end it again, the right way. Or start it again. Or perhaps I was groping for *anything* that would make me regard her the way I had blithely regarded her for years: As a sweet woman from back home who I could always turn to, and thus never would.

Not knowing why you make this call is a key part of the Nicole pathology.

You're lucky if you only make it once.

"Whoa . . . you," she said.

A long silence.

"I don't know whether I should let you go or not," I finally said.

Another key part of the Nicole pathology is thinking that your decision and desires are really the only ones that matter, and the fact that you're not a part of her thought-scape whatsoever is only a niggling obstacle.

"Look, I knew how you felt and it didn't matter," she said

to cut me, perhaps feeling entitled to it given the eight months of distance I had allowed since lambasting her.

Just a few seconds of talk. Neither mad nor forgiving nor resolving. Just talk. She was glad to hear I was doing all right. Click. She was gone. I gingerly replaced the phone onto its receiver.

I walked into the bathroom and looked in the mirror.

"That was it," I said to the imbecile.

"Now it's over, understand?" I commanded.

And it was.

8.

I regained control of normal life until December 25, 1997.

"Your father's gone," my mother said on the phone at 4:43 A.M.

Dad was two weeks shy of turning eighty-three—he was fifty-five when I was born—and he had been wallowing in a South Jersey hospital for four months, unresponsive and rarely awake. His third major stroke in nine years had taken all he had left.

Dying on Christmas day, forever cementing his memory on the holiday—at four in the frigging morning before one iota of Christmas could be enjoyed—was pure Dad. He loved attention. Even if—and occasionally especially if—it inconvenienced you. He was a good-looking Sicilian man, a barber, a late-life husband to a woman twenty years his junior. He was a worrier, a hypochondriac until the moment any treatment was suggested, and a mediocre thespian whenever he believed exaggerating his frailty might serve some aim.

Nearly comatose, tube-ridden and immobile, I thought he was done being Dad. But dying on Christmas, that was a sweet one. The coup de grâce. It had the unprosecutable possibility of randomness, and it morally demanded the benefit of the doubt given codes of societal politeness regarding the blameless dead. It was airtight.

But like him, I wouldn't have wanted it any other way.

My yearly opportunity to try to thoroughly enjoy Christmas despite his final masterpiece sort of keeps a tiny bit of our earthly contention alive, and this is how I most fully knew him.

Now there was the matter of the funeral, which would involve funeral-like happenings. And a brief reunion with Nicole.

9.

You have got to be kidding me, my last shred of better judgment lamented. *You're going to put your other hand into the blender?*

One more flight of imbecility involving Nicole was rationalized thusly:

Look around your father's casket. Fifty-three years of work, eight-two years of life, all those bums he dressed up at the shop so they could at least walk out straight-spined, crippled neighbors who got cuts and shaves for decades. Look who's here. Nobody. If he hadn't gotten married, got himself a wife, the net sum of everything would have been zero. It was the only lasting thing he ever did. Or maybe the only thing he ever did that, in the end, lasted.

Nicole came to the viewing and funeral. It needn't have been for me; my mother shared a friendship with her punctuated by a common interest in social work. In the day after my father's send off we took a ride in my car.

"You didn't talk to me for a year," she said.

"I can't stay mad at you," I replied.

In the next eight years, of the hundreds of forlorn dweebs who would tell me their Nicole stories, that line would inevitably be in half of them—the half that lost their minds and ran blindly into the abyss. You can't stay mad at Nicole because you never were actually mad at her, in the same way that you mistook livid indignation for some queer degree of love. (*Queer* as in "strange.") You were mad at yourself for being a pussy who was wrong for conjuring counterfeit feelings, wrong for ignoring them, wrong for acting on them—and just all–around wrong.

Two nights later, we were in my car in front of her house, after another "just as nice as ever there was" dinner.

To paraphrase Fitzgerald, I would now make the holocaust complete.

I launched into a curdling speech and professed my love for her, saying we (*we*) didn't want to find ourselves twenty years from now ruing a lost opportunity for eternal happiness.

It was more stomach wrenching than the car scene in *Chasing Amy*.

In the last second before I opened my mouth, the one lone dissenter in my mental Senate pleaded that the last fiber of human dignity demanded that we abort this kamikaze plan. He could then only watch in helpless horror. When I began my second minute, he put a finger down his throat, emptied his gut, and then swallowed the barrel of his sidearm and blew himself into a place where he would hear no more.

Meanwhile, Nicole was flushed with embarrassment.

"Nicole, my love for you is like a tiny baby bird. . . ."

The senator's eyes popped open on his half a head.

"You're holding this little bird in your hands. . . ."

I cupped her hands to demonstrate.

"You can let him live and grow, or you can decide to crush him . . . crush him and kill him."

I heard a second shot from the revolver.

Nicole looked at her cupped hands.

"Is he in there right now?" she asked.

"He is," I said.

"Now?" she said.

"Now." I said.

"Let me out! Let me out!" she baby-talked, trying to put some humor into this excruciatingly awkward folly. I stared at her, feeling the first twinge of regret for the staggeringly moronic feat I had just accomplished.

"I think I am sorry I said that to you," I said.

10.

Timing is everything.

The realization that I had committed extortion of a breathtaking degree, in hitting her with this right after my dad died, didn't dawn on me until weeks later.

"Man, you had her by the *tits*," a friend in Alaska observed. He was right. I might've gone down on Golda Meir had she cornered me in these circumstances.

In completing the well-worn Nicole arc of the plucky 50 percent who make this desperate play, she gave me the "we tried, it failed" talk after two tepid dates.

"The one who's not in love makes the tender speeches," I said to myself in the restaurant john right after she lopped me off. I had just bought a book with some Proust quotes.

"The night's young," she said after signing the death certificate of our stillborn dalliance in a festive Mexican joint. "Can we still do something?"

We saw *Titanic*.

Yes, it was.

CHAPTER THREE

The Old Flame

1.

"Where are you going to meet her?" Duane, my coworker, asked me in an Allentown sub shop almost two years after I had attempted to woo Nicole during the winter of my dad's demise.

"I don't know, somewhere in Philly. She asked me so she'll pick a place," I replied.

"Maybe it'll give you something for the column," he said.

By now, I had written a handful of my small dating dispatches, hot from the cauldron of my Allentown wanderings. That cauldron still contained Mimi, who I continued seeing infrequently enough that she, out of caution of being played, continued getting completely naked without ordering dessert. It also had a dash of Angela, a flight attendant six years older than me who showed that the skies could be friendly indeed.

Much had happened in the five months since Denis asked

me to jot down the basics of my social implosions. Greg, who had inherited the top editor spot after the long-time editor left, had been booted after ten months in the post. Dave, the previous director of the international editions of *Men's Health*, was installed as the chief editor. Denis withdrew shortly after the switch. All the Machiavellian suppositions of real and imagined intentions that follow any org-chart upheaval in any workplace were flying in grand fashion during those weeks.

Dave and the new creative director, Steve, liked the column, and it was upped from a box to a page. And I was upped in spirit from a grizzled, unnerved, and organizationally challenged editor to an inspired and organizationally challenged monthly columnist of the bigger, brighter dating column. A cartoon of me even ran on the page, though the illustrator didn't need to depict my bulbous face so literally. "*License*, man, take license," I pleaded. "Help the cause."

2.

"Every guy has one," Duane continued while we ate at the sub shop. "Every guy can relate to running into her."

Nicole had called me out of the blue two nights before and asked if I wanted to go to a Sicilian poetry reading and have dinner. Naturally this put thoughts in my head. Maybe she was going to throw herself at me and plead for forgiveness for being so stupid as to spurn me two years before. I was still dating the flight attendant—Angela—and in what touchy-feely therapists describe as a "good place." But as always, Angela was not white-veil material, and every little move she made was a clear message to that effect. She was free—as a bird, one could say—and would need a highly moneyed man with an offer of a significantly upgraded life to consider being grounded. Which was brilliantly fine with me.

But it still left Nicole's dusty spot vacant.

3.

Upon meeting Nicole in Philadelphia sitting through the poetry reading with her, and having dinner, I kept bracing for the sulphuric acid to rush through my innards and bring me back to that "bad place" I had known two years before.

When it didn't happen, I was astonished. Bewildered. Unless there was some huge mistake, the fabled metamorphosis had finally revealed itself.

I had gotten over her. Over her enough to know I was close to all the way.

Given that, whatever I had suffered on her account could not, in retrospect, have been as unbearable as I had made it out to be, I reasoned.

The only spike on the pain meter was bidding Nicole good night. There had been no exchange of pheromones in our outing, as usual, as nature and fate had ordained. I put my hands in my back pockets upon saying goodbye, so my lean to kiss her wouldn't become a grasp, so a foolish grasp wouldn't become a foolish test of muscle memory. She came close to me; unafraid since she had never been in real or mistaken love, and kissed me in the way you kiss someone whom you know had once wanted to kiss you as anything but a friend. I hugged her hard, lifting her, telling her with my grip that if this was the last time I saw her . . . well, I wished it wouldn't be. But if it was, it was, since we had little actual reason to keep in contact. And my track record in keeping friends, even uncomplicated friends, was deplorable. I hated God and nature for making us unworkable. It wouldn't have been any skin off anyone's ass to have it be different.

And, just like that, she was gone. Again.

4.

"Jesus," came the typed reply from Steve.

He liked the column I'd written about my brief reunion with Nicole. The Old Flame. (In fitting Nicole-story fashion, even my title was a cliché.) Readers responded to it; in the following months and years, a potful of men sent their own Nicole anecdotes to me via e-mail, and dozens of Nicoles chimed in as well, giving the often wrenching—and occasionally indifferent—view from the other foxhole. The Old Flame circulated on the net and on relationship bulletin boards, and in time hundreds of people mentioned the column to me. Via the miracle of the perpetual junk drawer called the Internet, people occasionally still bring it up.

Nicole never did.

CHAPTER FOUR

Making It

1.

At the bustling Sterling Hotel Bar on Hamilton Street, Allentown, late, Mimi was drunk as hell.

"Where have you been?" she said.

"Around, just . . ." Luckily a deafening round of whoops from the next room broke above the deafening music from the cover band.

It was one of those rare nights that you harbor tiny expectations for every night you go out. The one that defeats the 95 percent of reality for most single guys, which is that almost every night you go out is going to be exactly the same. You go out searching for something to happen, waiting for something to happen, thinking something is continually about to happen, and then going home feeling either a little or a lot like a jerk, depending on how much cash you blew and how close you believe something came to actually happening.

This night, however, was one of the Golden Nights. A Sinatra Night. The kind in which you go out alone for a beer, find a gaggle of friends at the bar, including a small pride of single girls, at least one of which has an established and not yet dead history with you.

This can happen three times in a week, and then not happen again for five years. But once it happens, you're quite sure that your spell of banality has been broken and such nights will now greet you every time you open a pub door.

Pub doors make frustrating Skinner box levers.

2.

"You're creepily cute," Anna said, also drunk, while being jostled by the crowd in the Sterling.

I'll take it.

"He isn't so unattractive, right?" Tina said, adding her vote. Her tone made me suspect that they had discussed me before. But of course they had.

I was beaming.

"Back at—"

"Shush!" Tina said, looking at me, swaying, sipping her Yuengling.

"Kiss me."

I looked at her.

"God, why now? Mimi is *right there*," I whispered.

Mimi was watching us with lasered drunken eyeballs. Then she fell into me in a faked tipsy stagger.

"Hello," I said merrily, like an ambassador of good times

and testosterone. Anna gulped her beer and turned away into the crowd. *Mimi had better not ruin this night*, I thought.

"You're staying, aren't you?" Tina asked, raising her voice. "Meet us in the back bar," she yelled.

"The back bar," I repeated, nodding. Tina, tall and German, made herself small, holding her beer to her tight top, and slipped away.

"Let's *go*," Mimi said.

I pretended not to hear her. This was a pickle. I was the designated sure hookup talent with a pressing engagement fifty feet in the back bar, and had drunk, sexy Mimi hanging on me and ready to go. And I had only been at the bar for ten minutes. God knows what other options would certainly develop in the next hour.

Jesus, I thought, *I love Allentown.*

It's only Friday, I reasoned. *Go with Mimi now, find those other girls tomorrow night. They're not going anywhere. There's no need to be greedy when this will happen every single time I venture into a bar from now on.*

With Mimi percolating in the passenger seat, I realized there had been a distinct change in my behavior in the last month. With the calling card of my dating column, and the accompanying need—and expectation from others—to have at least one encounter a month with at least one female that was story-worthy for 1.7 million guys, I was operating with a new mode of confidence. This was in contrast to the courtship M.O. I had followed—with rare punishing exception—since sixth grade, which could be summed up as, "don't be an ass."

My new, more confident Plan B—which was a swaggering,

act-now-think-later mode—was paying dividends. I had col-
lected four phone numbers and two e-mails in the last two weeks,
from the grade of women I would typically stalk for nine to fifteen months before deciding they weren't worth the trouble.

I had not actually called any of the women who gave me
their phone numbers, since I was mentally playing one off the
other. With this pool of choices, I rationalized that the two
women who seemed most likely to have nothing interesting to
say didn't deserve to be called. Then five days elapsed, and
calling the third woman and trying to remind her who I was
became an easy chore to put off. I probably allowed this delay
because I was engaging in some lovely e-mail flirting with
Diana, an artist and part-time waitress (this sounded familiar)
who showed herself to be a discerning and self-respecting
woman by refusing to give me her phone number when I
asked after nine minutes of small talk, and gave me her e-mail
address instead.

The mother of my children can't be a reckless fool.

3.

"So where have you beennnn?" Mimi said, sliding her left
hand between my thighs as we drove to her apartment.

"Around. I've had a lot of late nights at work."

"When you stopped calling I thought I had done something wrong."

"What? No," I said, cueing the radio therapist. "Of course
not. Not at all. No. I'm just weird that way."

"I need to get out of this town!" she screamed with drunk-
blubbering tears, banging her fists repeatedly against her fore-

head. She startled me so much I nearly careened into oncoming traffic.

4.

"It's desserrrrt timmme," she baby-talked, completely naked except for flip-flops she had inexplicably fished onto her feet before leading me to her bedroom. Heretofore we had always stopped at coffee rather than enjoying the long-billed desert while canoodling on her carpet or couch. The bedroom was new territory.

Mimi was on her back, my chin above her ribs, tousling my scalp hairs with her painted fingers. Her phone rang. It was four in the morning. She arched back with her right hand and picked up the receiver.

"Fuck you!" she screamed and threw the handset against the wall.

"Your mother?" I said a few seconds later.

"Him!" she said. She cried and banged her cranium like she did in my Geo Prizm. Which no longer had a golf club in its trunk, I remembered.

"Is *this* the price of being beautiful?!"

"*Well?*" she yelled when I didn't say anything.

"Mimi, I wouldn't really know—"

"Why are you just laying there?!" she screamed. "*Why?!* I hate this town! *I hate this town!* I'm gonna get out!"

More head abuse.

This wasn't turning out well.

"Mimi, about dessert and all, I don't really think it's a goo—"

"Are you *crazy?!* You're not here for me! You're not around!"

There was a long, long minute of silence.

"No, I'm not. You are correct." I caressed the tortuous artwork on her arm. "You look tired and your cat here wants to . . . I'm going to go now."

"Don't go! Not yet."

Three more minutes passed. I caressed her arm, wondering if her ex was crashing through the last speed bump in the far condo parking lot.

Mimi lifted up her leg and arched her foot in the moonlight. Her vagina looked back at me like an Edvard Munch painting.

"I'm wearin' flip-flips," she announced.

"Okay, I'm going to go now," I said.

"Not yet!" she screamed. She grabbed my head hairs and breathed harder, looking intently at her levitated foot, suffering bed spins. She turned to me and blinked her eyes. Then back up at her foot.

"Ready for the beach," she baby-talked.

5.

It was 5:20 A.M. before she fell asleep and I got out of there, driving home in the dank morning dew like a broken fool.

"I gotta get out of this town," I said to myself, deciding that I had driven back this way down Hamilton Street at least 92,000 times in the last five years and eight months, wearing a groove of alcoholic homesick boredom punctuated by nights out with Greg, who was gone, and long lunches with the guys at *Men's Health* who made up my proxy family, who dissipated to their actual families or Princeton or Philly or Elizabeth or wherever come darkness and weekends. I was thirty and thinking about buying a house—*buying a house*—and putting down roots in Allentown for no other reason than it seemed the responsible thing for a graying thirty-year-old to do.

If I have to drive back down Hamilton Street once more, to make it 92,001 times, I decided, *I will plunge my Geo Prizm and myself off the nearest bridge into the Lehigh River.*

I knew that it was only a matter of time before I would find myself driving out of a bar parking lot at 2:00 A.M., just as intoxicated as everyone else on the road, stopping for cheese fries at the Queen City Diner, and then—instead of driving by it as every man with the faintest reason to live will do—making the fatal choice of pulling into the dilapidated nudie shack under the 78 bridge. And that would be the moment at which a single man crosses the precipice from the land of living into the realm of being the hopeless, unloved joke that only exists to serve as a warning to others who still have time to save themselves.

I might stop at the dilapidated nudie shack tomorrow night, I shuddered. *I might do it in five years.* But it was waiting for me. Beckoning its dark come-hither with a glued-on fingernail.

"It might be time to start thinking about a change," I said sighing, as I watched a broken red light on Hamilton Street flicker against the morning sky like a tracer bullet.

6.

"It's a new magazine from the AARP," a woman on the phone named Helen said with a American-habituated British accent. "A colleague of yours said that you may be someone we should talk to."

Whether you're as happy as a shit-swimming pig in your job, or miserable, or lockstepping at one of the usual points in between, you want to get a call like this. Inside all men, connected to the tiny eternal flame of faith regarding your prospects for finding love or maintaining a nonhostile coexistence with a woman—with all the thousands of consequentials that brings—there's a fat tube running to a gas tank with a fill gauge that has an orange pin hovering between "E" and "$."

Helen's call was a highway sign on the outskirts of a pleasant but isolated town, surrounded by a harsh desert, that read, *Just in case you think you've seen just about everything you're going to see here, and just possibly want to hazard moseying on, we're pleased to privately inform you that there's a NEW service station with slightly DIFFERENT AMENITIES 400 miles ahead.*

My Prizm got exactly 399 miles to the tank.

7.

The anguish and ecstasy of leaving *Men's Health* after nigh five years felt like an amputation and an ejaculation. I was now as enthusiastic about bringing more regurgitated exercise tips into the world as I was about driving down Hamilton Street, though the diversion of the dating column had rejuvenated my occupational jollies for a precious few days out of the month. Loyalty was another wrench. I had not only started my magazine staffer experience there—after an editor named Jeff decided to roll the dice and hope that hiring an unknown quantity like myself wouldn't be his professional undoing—I had been fostered and tolerated. I'm all about being fostered and tolerated. I don't think there's anything else a man can ask from the earth. Had I been Thomas Jefferson, I would have lined out that asinine grandiosity of "life, liberty, and the pursuit of happiness" and quilled in "fostered and tolerated" without a second thought.

Being fostered and tolerated in Allentown, Pennsylvania, seventy-two miles and one universe from my hometown near Jersey's nipple at the flank of south Philly, however, had run its course. I knew every bartender and every server and every manager and every regular in every one of the nine bars, if not by name at least by their unshaven faces (broads included) and I had a sneaking fear that tipping 20 percent and sending over friendly pints might not spur any of them to lay a rose on my casket on some forthcoming rainy afternoon.

And the AARP job paid pretty well.

8.

It wasn't until I had accepted the features job at this new mag, called *My Generation*, that I learned that the name AARP, which I recollected from having heard at some point in my life stood for "American Association of Retired Persons," no longer stood for that. Mainly because Americans in their fifties can't retire anymore. It was some weeks after that when I learned

that AARP also no longer stood for AARP, but was now officially only pronounced phonetically as *arp*. I suppose they did
this because they had decided to kill the anachronistic words
behind the acronym, but still needed to keep the acronym because people knew it. A parallel might be if the Central
Intelligence Agency suddenly decided they would no longer
involve themselves with intelligence, but they still wanted to
keep their CIA stationery, and thus announced that they
would henceforth be known as *see-ah*.

The new arp magazine, which was only sent to the four or
five million youngsters aged fifty to fifty-five in their gargan-
tuan database of ripening citizens who paid a few dollars a
year to get wheelbarrows of weekly junk mail and save 15 percent on their next car rental, had two winning perks. First and
foremost, they'd relocate me (or, in my view at the time, locate
me) to New York City from Allentown. Secondly, the new
lifestyle mag was being top-edited by Betsy Carter, a legendarily venerable and well-known editor who had done stints
at *Esquire*, *Newsweek*, and scads of other pubs in a long career,
and I figured I'd learn something new from her.

Dave, the new editor at *Men's Health*, liked my dating column enough to ask me to continue writing it even if I wasn't
going to be on the staff any longer—which twisted a fostered-
and-tolerated dagger into my heart, since writing gigs like
that aren't often kept alive for defectees. The handsome sum
he offered to pay me to keep doing it salted the dagger, since
much of the extra ching coming from the arp raise was going
to be swallowed by the peculiarly oppressive Manhattan expense called living; my monthly rent of 870 dollars for a two-

bedroom, three-bath condo in Allentown would be traded up to 2,500 dollars for a studio apartment on Fifty-seventh Street in which my bed and living room couch would have to touch each other.*

9.

Moving to New York disrupted the newly tested chutzpah of my Plan B, since the familiar environment and peoples of Allentown were no doubt contributors to the recent swell in my testicles. But the news of moving gave me something semi-interesting to talk about with the few women that I had established a minor repartee within the last three months— Tina, Anna, and Amy.

Within two months of my settling in New York in March 2001, all three had visited my new horrifically expensive room just under Columbus Circle. And I was visiting, briefly and knowingly temporarily, a phase of both life transition and dizzying grand luck in which these strange circumstances of change and active relationships had let me—in one sudden rush—walk onstage and participate in the full-Technicolor action of life, with all of its beautifully interesting and distracting emergencies and sensations, instead of continuing to be a numb and hopeful observer.

*If my dad had ever glimpsed the notion that someone could—and then separately decided that they would—pay that kind of money to live in a small apartment, anywhere, without being forced to do it by the Mob, I think he would have probably envisioned the diapered man-child suffering from profound mental retardation that we sadly watched eat a hamburger roll in Bob's Big Boy in 1985, and then envisioned him having his own checkbook.

My dating columns sprang off my fingers in the spring and summer of '01; Tom, my editor rarely changed much.

As dating just one woman had always been my definition of cup-runneth-over, I soon allowed Tina and Anna to drift away. They knew each other well, so I was more relieved than sorry that they didn't stick around.

Amy, however, I did not want to let go.

She was a twenty-two-year-old artist living in Allentown, and I can only assume she waited tables somewhere without telling me, since the vocational makeup of my last four near-serious romantic targets had been queerly similar. She was a petite, pale, Irish-Mexican girl with a body too beautiful for her own good, and a light, reluctant laugh that I had almost no power to elicit. I had written about one of our dates in an early column—in which we got pulled over driving to her apartment after dinner and I nearly got a DUI—and she was, to quote her, "not happy."

"I mentioned that I was wearing a thong, but I did *not* show you my thong, and that is *not* what made you swerve," she said tersely.

In the life a thirtyish single man who sees dates as sparsely spaced foot rocks in a wide, icy pond, when in the company of a girl like Amy along a dark stretch of lonely Pennsylvania road, a mentioned thong, an imagined thong, and a seen thong are all quite transferable phases of energy.

"You might be right, and I'm sorry," I said to her on the phone. "You're not wearing it right now, are you?"

10.

As we laid on my bed in my Fifty-seventh Street apartment, late in the evening, I kissed Amy's forehead and told her that I was, to put it mildly, happy that she had come. And happy that she had stayed. I felt an ease with her, an affection, an erotic hunger, and a cautiously genuine belief and hope that all were not going to blow to smithereens at any moment or decay.

That isn't every day.

"Will you promise me one thing?" she asked. "Will you not write about us?"

"Why not?"

"Because," she said.

I was silent. Or I softly said yes. Or, more softly, no. I remember doing all three, depending on what I wish to remember. But mostly I remember smelling her skin.

As with the thong and winding road, we can only remember, and memory makes it so.

CHAPTER FIVE

The Net Frenzy

1.

To keep the dating column fodder coming, I needed to have at least three dates a month; that was my only sure way of experiencing at least one good social incident that I could extrapolate into a thematic essay of 890 words.

And keep my promise, or expressed intention, or acknowledgment of some expressed preference, to Amy.

With her being in Allentown and me being in New York, we surely weren't going steady, I believed. (If people still say "going steady.") I knew she had a bevy of suitors at each of the nine bars, since I had been one and watched others chat her up and down. Men threw money at her. Chefs offered her free chow, and more.

It's a beautiful girl's prerogative.

Whatever we were going to be would be slow in solidifying. Amy wasn't going to endure loneliness in Allentown, and

I wasn't going to ask her to move into my 575-square-foot mansion, and she was making noises about moving back to Toledo.

Allentown could make you miss Toledo, I guess.

2.

To fill my column quota, online dating Web sites looked to be a promising resource.

It's like laying crab traps.

You set the bait, go sleep or eat or drink beer, and just wait. Then you go back the next morning and see what good fortune has waiting for you.

This was my immediate take on Internet dating sites.

Well, not my first immediate take. When I tried a few early fledgling dating sites in 1997, they were hopelessly arcane, filled with tech nerds who rarely posted photos, and otherwise not for general consumption. By 2001, however, things had changed.

Match.com was the über site[*] then, as now. I signed up, put up a profile, and within a week I was e-mailing six different women. I found that the bravado necessary to engage Plan B was far easier to muster and maintain when you didn't actually have to deal with a woman face-to-face. You write something witty and boldly audacious in your Plan B–ish sounding profile, or transmit a shot of Plan B–grade confidence in an e-mail to a honey with a nice photo (which is hopefully her;

[*]More people say über with annoying frequency now. Didn't we beat the Krauts in '45?

I have been duped on occasion), and then wait for positive responses.

Since you know the women on the sites are single and looking (usually), and you can glean enough info in their profile to concoct thoughtful-sounding, relevant questions ("Do you enjoy working with meth addicts?"), getting an initial positive response isn't too hard for most men who aren't sexual predators, don't look like warthogs, and have a couple of brain cells available to craft innocuous e-mails. And negative responses? Nothing is quite so merciful as being shot down without hurtful effect, to butcher Winston Churchill's famous sentiment. Unless you counter one of the relatively few sadistically polite women who *insist* on responding to your note with a "you seem nice, but I don't think we're a match" Deny-O-Gram, you might forget that you even e-mailed the chick. You're being rejected and you don't know why or care!

For those who appreciate the difference, that's a boon.

3.

Terri. Dolores. Victoria. Kim. Danielle. Liza. Carole. Grace. Elizabeth. Carla. Linda. Nikki. Marina. Katie. Brenda. Faiza. Mary-Ann. Ginger. (Not kidding). Amy (another Amy). Aimee.

These were the ones that lasted at least three dates. The once-and-doners numbered several dozen.

Within five months of first going online, I had been on seventy-six dates. Within a year I had tallied 112.

Many of the women I met, especially the once-and-doners, had blown this pace away.

"I go on three dates a week almost every week," said Sallie, a twenty-four-year-old great-looking blonde from Hoboken. "If I have no money I might do more, since I get nice dinners."

"Do you want me to buy you dinner?" I asked. We were having two glasses of red wine.

"No," she said, laughing. "I'm not being a dinner whore tonight."

"A dinner whore?"

While this term seemed to be the exact quid-pro-quo arrangement men have been hoping to establish since the first caveman offered a grubby root from his dirty hand, Sallie explained that she meant a woman who wrings a few expensive dinners out of a guy by making him think she's going to put out, but then decides she's tired/it's too soon/they're just not soulmates/he's getting pushy/etc. when her belly's full.

"Do you want me to buy you dinner?" I asked.

Hey, you gotta try. Just as women who'll sleep with a guy for five dollars and five million dollars are the same thing, a shot in a million is still a shot.

4.

I was on Match.com an hour a day at the office. And three hours at night. Soon I was switching on the computer when I got up to piss at 4:00 A.M. just to see if any women—and which ones—answered my e-mails or finally relented and sent a note to the guy behind this irresistibly confident write-up.

When it reached five hours a day online, with identical

profiles on Match.com, Lavalife.com, Nerve.com, and two New York–only sites, I had to look in the mirror and make an estimation of what I had become.

Addict was never a term that insulted me, whether it was being thrown my way for food, punishment, sleeping, procrastination, wasting money, you name it. Booze was the only reference that chaffed me.

But I was most certainly an online dating addict, if the DSM-IV definition of "addict" had any merit whatsoever.

I knew what I had to do.

"How can I spend more time online dating while making it look like less?" I wondered.

The addiction to shopping for women on online dating sites, and—to a lesser extent—actually meeting a portion of those women every other day for an interminable period, really doesn't need to be explained since its core motivation is obvious. But some people think it's frivolous so I'll give a few details on it.

Naturally, there's the draw of the serendipity of having a new, strange woman drop into your life via your e-mail inbox at any moment, and freely stoke your internal flame of faith that you won't die inside a cardboard box in a church parking lot. This happens without you having to go anywhere, spend anything, or, really, do jack. And this comes with the rare added security and risk-free quality of having her approach you.

Above that, there was the sea of smiles and brown eyes and blue eyes and dimples and suggestive smirks staring back at you from hundreds of little thumb-photos on your computer screen, all belched forth within four seconds of launching a Boolean search. And unlike women in magazine photos, these chicks actually existed and could be contacted. Instantly. And unlike women who pass in front of you in the flesh every day, these were self-qualified prospects who, at the very basic least, were telling you straight-up that they were single, available, and actively looking for a guy. And quite possibly so hard up that they'd jump on you. They were readily making small talk with you via their profile essays, giving you enough info to visualize their traits and vulnerabilities, teasing you into gauging their odds of (1) being that one-in-a-trillion broad who was put on earth for the sole purpose of answering your tragically fucked-up needs, or (2) being an extremely hot woman with such severe low self-esteem issues that she would love to be your Alice for as long as it gratified you.

Completing the alien strangeness of this opportunity, there are dozens and dozens and dozens of these women. A great many. All staring back at you plaintively, or with expressions that are easily imagined as plaintive. Their plentiful numbers give you a smug option of reading their little no-risk small-talk pitches in their written essays and then, if it suits you, opting for the potential satisfaction of saying "Good God, screw off" and moving on to the next thumbnail photo.

Importantly, the online dating addiction was not fueled (at least not predominantly) by looking at each of those smirks and dimples and smiles and thinking, "I could have sex with you, or you, or you, or you, or you, or you, or . . ." That went without saying. Online dating can be an efficient vehicle for serial sex, if you want to use it for that—but the normal single guy who's never put anyone under with horse tranquilizers and is just a smidge socially inept isn't using online dating sites for this chief purpose. Or if he were, he wouldn't stick to

dancing with the "nice girls" in the general membership of
Match.com. Escort services would be cheaper and require listening to far less inane chatter about evil conspiracies in the
office and "why my life sucks" philosophies. Or he'd use one
of the many sites with a "looking for some spicy fun with the
right person(s)" option, including the ubiquitous Craigs list,
rather than only the sites that mainly attracts white-picket-
fence dreamers.

More accurately stated, I would look at each of the those
smirks and dimples and smiles and think, "You could be a
new life, or you could be a new life, or you . . ."

I wasn't shopping for a low-maintenance meat sleeve who
would accessorize my life; maybe that comes in your fifties or
sixties when you're a thrice-divorced forsaken loser and
every last atom of idealism has gone the way of confidence in
government. I was looking for the transformational Virgin
Mary (who, of course, was instinctually a hellcat in bed). This
woman would storm into my doleful existence and blow out
all of the snot that takes the form of petty, ancillary, life-wasting
worries. She'd install herself—with my consent and to my sal-
vation—as my singular beacon of concern, and gatekeeper of
all effluvia that might otherwise badger me.[*]

This could happen in our first week together. After that, if
she just took away the worries of sex and isolation and social
services removing the tykes, and freed me up enough to con-
centrate on work and tinker with my '68 Ford Falcon in the
garage on the occasional nice afternoon, I'd be happy.

---

[*]I'm still taking applications from females to fill this position.

5.

"Are you going to take down your profile?" Carla asked. "I mean, I happened to notice that you still had it up yesterday."

This was our fourth date.

I should take it down, I reasoned. Carla was nice. A law student. A girlfriend–candidate if ever one existed. I wasn't going to do better than her in the next ten hours, most likely. Thinking on this, and my online dating addiction that I carefully hid from her—though she may have been a junkie of a far higher order, for all I suspected—I realized why my profile was not coming down. Was *never* coming down. So help me God.

As were most participants, I later learned, I wasn't using online dating to find, I was using online dating to look.

Looking brought in dating column stories by the promising bagfull. And I needed dating column content, not a steady squeeze who might be all squeezed out of worthwhile journalistic fodder in three weeks.

Secondly, since the options in online dating were limitless, the possibilities were limitless, and each individual woman's fitness and capacity to be my one and only was badly undermined by the possibility that a better mate was just one more search away.

The idiocy of proclaiming the process successfully concluded—I have found *her* and may now search no more forever—seemed antithetical to the whole reality of online dating. Moving from the off-line logistical constraints of geography, time, chance, and connectivity in dating ("Ron, you really ought to meet my roommate's sister, Meg") to the vast, boundless freedom and incalculable spoils of plenty online ("I'm Tara from Fort Sumter and I can meet you in New York this Saturday") meant the spoils could only be enjoyed as long as you kept working the process. Stopping, taking down your profile for just one woman would be a bit like killing the golden goose because it had just shat you out a nice Elgin watch.

6.

"Carla, please don't call any more," I told her three weeks later, after ducking her with limited success. I was a bloodshot wreck. I had just completed eleven coffee, wine or dinner dates with women I had met online in fourteen days, a net shelling of at least six hundred dollars from my bank account and not one of them was remotely worth a second date—five by virtue of indicating that they would absolutely not be open to the prospect, through dismissive body language and droned speech. This was one taxing peril of meeting people through online dating sites, one that you learn is a big part of the game very quickly: great profile, pretty good-looking photo, witty and engaging e-mail banter, maybe even a promising phone call. Then you show up in Panchito's on MacDougal Street and the entity waiting for you is a halitosic troll who belongs to a witch coven, or overtly, instantly and phantasmically disappointed in what you've brought to the table (which is even worse if she's a halitosic troll), or is a fun date who just might—might—be that transformational Virgin Mary with Alice potential, and who gives you a squeeze-hug good-bye and then never returns another e-mail or phone call.

Carla had become a lingering taxing peril.

"We're not right for each other," I told her.

She had called five times during my two weeks of eleven dates, and while I had thought the radio therapist had laid it out pretty clearly when Carla and I had talked last, when he said, "We're not right for each other, Carla," the next day brought an invitation to a Halloween party. And then the offer of a spare theater ticket her boss had given her. And then a voice message just to see how I was doing.

I felt like a beautiful girl.

"I'm sorry that you won't even give it a chance, because you seemed interested," Carla said.

Yes, I had seemed interested, I wanted to tell her. I had seemed interested because, hell, I might have had cause to become interested. Had our third date had the caliber of conversation of our first date—which is nary possible since first-date conversation is often a standard script of time-tested anecdotes and A-list biographical ditties ("My middle name is from a Hall and Oates song. . . ."). Had our physical chemistry panned out to sexual chemistry, had she asked me even one frigging question about me or my life amidst her sweet and witty monologues regarding her ambitions and character-filled family, I may have become interested.

It happens this way in dating, and she knew it as well as I did. It was nothing personal. And that was much of the problem.

"You led me on," she said, coldly. "If you weren't interested, why did you almost sleep with me?"

"Ah! *Ah-hahh!*" I yelled in the receiver. "I knew you were going to throw that in my face. That's why I didn't sleep with you, Carla. Oh, you'd really be tearing into me with some self-righteous bullshit if we *had* had sex, wouldn't you?"

7.

As any amateur Freud could spot in reviewing my sexual history, and as also evidenced in my malingering tryst with Mimi, I have a fear of intercourse that runs wide and selective, if not deep and well-placed. Identifying its origin is not hard.

The first branding came in the late seventies, in fifth grade, when an ill-conceived, ill-taught, experimental sex-ed class in my grammar school left me with the knowledge that I had been given VD by my mom.

Mr. Jeffers, the permed-haired gym teacher who had decided some years before that leading ten-year-olds through jumping jacks and hitting on fresh-faced elementary-ed cuties was preferable to wading in the leech-filled swamps of Cambodia, gave his lesson on venereal disease to the fifth grade boys, segregated in one classroom while the girls were given starter tampons in another. He explained that sex brought forth babies, which was covered in about two minutes. The next forty-three minutes were dedicated to VD.

Jeffers explained that VD—all or any VD, which was just to be known as VD—made you feel like you were peeing fire. It caused festering sores on your dong that could make it drop off, and cause your brain to become riddled with holes, and your lips to sprout weeping, pus-oozing boils that would make people banish you to some sort of concentration camp. Then you'd die in your late teens or twenties without ever having kissed a girl, or gotten to touch her tit or finger her. VD was also completely incurable and untreatable. Almost all girls had VD, or any of them could and would have it, and a dirty lady would not only infect you but also infect her fetuses, which were born through her vagina and not her belly button although yes that would be far more logical but nonetheless was not the case, and then her fetuses would have the same short and horrid life.

This was my take-home of his verbatim talk.

After the class, I tugged on his velour tracksuit and asked Jeffers the one thing that didn't make perfect, horrifying sense to me. I understood that dirty ladies were the root of all earthly evil, but how did a woman get VD in the first place?

He smiled lecherously, then with a twinge of resentment.

"By having sex too many times," he said.

I mulled this while trodding the four blocks home.

There was me, my brother, my sister, my other sister. And God knows how many other times they did it. It burned when I peed, now that I thought of it. I stopped dead on Salem Street, bit my knuckle in terror, looked around to see who saw me, who already knew, and felt tears explode out of my disease-ridden eyeballs. I ran home wailing inside, sprinted up the stairs to my room, slammed the door and begged God to give me one more chance, to wipe clean my slate of sin and disgrace and give me one more chance.

"What's wrong?" my mom asked.

The unadulterated nerve.

Reluctantly, I let it be known.

"I got VD!" I screamed.

She wanted to know how this came to happen. That was rich. Really rich.

"I got it from you," I hissed, thrusting my soon to be chancre-ridden index finger at her.

Again, she wanted details. I pointed at each kid's photo on

the piano, and then at my sixty-four-year-old father, who was reading the paper in the kitchen.

"And God knows how many other times!" I cried. I reminded her about the fetuses infection scourge that she might have considered had she cared. And then I reiterated the soiling seminal evil that caused the VD and had ruined my life, courtesy of her.

"Jeffers said you get it from having sex too many times!"

"Not with the same person!" she shot back.

Immediately after dinner I was back upstairs conferencing God, and I thanked him for seeing fit to handle my request. He had granted me clemency on this extremely big deal, and I promised him that I would never take the gift of being VD-free for granted.

The residual gratitude I have for this charity is probably one reason I don't look fondly on frivolous intercourse, and perhaps the reason why reading the back of a condom box can send me rocking in the corner, hugging my knees and frothing saliva.

The second seed of my coitaphobia likely dates to my sophomore year of high school, when I resolved that I was going to pick up Sarah Zancosky, a freshman from a nearby high school who had such legendarily enormous breasts that her last name became an adjective and a euphemism.* She hung out, and was to be found, at the dirt stretch behind the King of Pizza pizza-parlor parking lot on Route 130, where we all loitered on Friday and Saturday nights in hoards of anywhere from twenty-five to three hundred, teens without a

---

*You might have said, "So I'm talking to her, and she's got these Zancosky-sized melons in my face . . ." or "Nice Zancoskies!" or "Dude, I saw them, Yvonne's are great but they're not Zancoskies," and the like.

piazza or a gymnasium or anywhere else they could legally be together exercising our animal right to be together in hoards, with primered and Bondo-dappled Chevelles and Novas and Chargers and Belvederes and Fairlanes and Camaros and Monte Carlos from the sixties idling and peeling around us, and one '68 Ford Falcon parked on the grass. It was a short-lived slice of *American Graffiti* in Gloucester, New Jersey, complete with the last era of leaded-gas muscle cars with bench seats and grumbling Detroit 277s, 350s, and 351s spitting out pure carbon-filled exhaust. I often wonder if contemporary high school guys sit on the hoods of their Honda Civics and Nissan Sentras in pizza-joint parking lots now, muttering low taunts to each other like "41 mpg, motherfucker."

I was going to pick up Sarah Zancosky for three reasons.

One, I was in a funk that led to testing an early iteration of the willy-nilly confident Plan B, so I believed I could. Two, she didn't go to my high school (I went to a regional school, so kids who lived twenty-nine miles away were my classmates, while kids who lived six blocks away—but over the district line   and hung out at the King of Pizza pizza-parlor parking lot were not), so the leprosy of rejection would not follow me into my daily school life. Three, she didn't go to my high school, so showing up with her— her and those must-be-seen-to-be-believed Zan-coskies—in front of my high school crowd would change my reputation in a more stunning and permanent way than snaring a girl in my own circle who could later plead insanity.

I only had Sarah's best interests in mind, really.

"Dad, I've met this girl named Sarah Zancosky at the King of Pizza parking lot and I'm gonna go out with her," I told my seventy-one-year-old father. "Look at her."

I have no idea where I swiped her wallet-sized school picture from, but it showed just enough of her to show she was a Zancosky.

"What do you think?" I asked.

He was silent, nonplussed. He typically responded with bland, noncommittal, generalized, half-comprehended discussion-ending positivity when I asked him anything—along the lines of "How about that?" Anything else might have thrown me into a rage or required more difficult, discussion-lengthening thought, or otherwise have emphasized the large gap between a tired seventy-one-year-old man and a roiling teen he had foolishly sired.

So this reaction was odd.

"What do I think?" he said. "I'll tell you what I think. You met this girl in a parking lot and she's going to go out with you? I'll tell you what I think. She's pregnant and she's going to blame you!"

My mouth flew ajar. Since this was the only hint of a sex talk he had ever given me, and one of the very few distinct, indictable opinions he had ever expressed on any issue solely regarding my life, I was staggered. DNA tests weren't household knowledge in 1986, much less 1936 when he had likely last revised his own bylaws of rational recklessness, so his warning seemed plausible. It cut deep.

When Sarah Zancosky hastily called me an hour before our date the following day and said she had to tend to an allegedly sick aunt, I didn't press her.

These two die-stamped incidents, carved deeper by coming of age in the eighties and nineties and when HIV added a new category of merriness to the STD repertoire (as well as,

watching my share of peers have their lives derailed by acci-
dental reproduction) may have something small to do with
my disinclination to copulate unless I'm genuinely fairly attracted to the dirty—er, lady. And even then, having inherited
my father's penchant for grand mal worrying doesn't lead my
subconscious to cheerlead for the "do her now!" decision, at
least when I'm not presented with the opportunity immediately before me.

Finally, to a small degree, I've been burned before. A broken condom once ruined my life for a full two weeks.

My father's message was clear, and he was not a misogynist:[*]
If you give a questionable woman the power to accuse you of
something, or exploit you as a stereotypically guilty man for her
own gain, she can devastate you and it'll be your fault.

8.

Carla was now lending a quiet legitimacy to my fear of
having sex with near-strangers—and people who may reveal
themselves to be near-strangers—and I wanted to throttle her
for it. It was the last thing I needed.

"That's one reason I didn't have sex with you, Carla, and
one reason I wouldn't," I said. "I knew you were going to
throw it my face if I did."

"I'm truly sorry for you," she said.

My would-be stalker receded.

But I wasn't nearly done with the Net.

---

[*]I am not a misogynist whatsoever, though very occasionally I have been ac-
cused of being one by some goddamned bitch.

CHAPTER SIX

Watching the Carnival

1.

Landing in New York meant changing my social arena, which in Allentown had been growing predictably Allentownish due to the distasteful effort it would involve to seek out more excitement there. Aside from art-making waitresses, my lone cohorts in Allentown were the small handful of people I knew from the lone, strangely located publishing company I worked for. I was something of a goldfish in a prairie pond, with a couple of other goldfish scattered about.

New York was different. Tired pond metaphors aside, it is a particularly easy place for a goldfish to eat himself to death.

The clique of magazine publishing people in Manhattan is larger than the one in Allentown, in case anyone ever wants a direct answer to that question. There was also a small cadre of Allentown expats who had made this journey before me, and they offered ready company. Taking a magazine writer or editor out of a small town and plopping him (or, more often, her) into Manhattan caused me to notice an odd juxtaposition, one that was no doubt happening in myself.

If you're a young magazine staffer in a small Pennsylvania city, the vast majority of people don't know who you are and don't care. Perhaps due to the workaday humility of the surroundings, you tend to feel that this is a proper response to one human's existence. But when you're a young magazine staffer in New York City, the vast majority of people don't know who you are and don't care, and this, in tiny moments, might make you want to tear your skin off your face.

This has quite a bit to do with that idiosyncratic recipe of the people mill that churns out magazine writers and editors (as discussed in Chapter 1). I suspect it also happens to some degree in every vocation, from pet supplies to auto parts, due to New York's special way of trumpeting the greatness of the individual by celebrating humanity as a noble mass of inconsequential fleas. But there's also the quasi-glamour factor involved in glossy publishing, which perfectly suits those budding magaziners who spent their high school years wearing cheap sneakers and thinking "Revenge will be mine." The glamour factor comes from exactly three things: (1) Magazines involve photography, (2) your actual name is printed somewhere in the pub in thousands or millions of copies every month, and (3) you're continually accosted by people who want to use you to get something—and at least half of these people are comely babies who want to become magaziners because of 1 and 2.

Groupies.

Well, not exactly groupies. They smile at you, wait in long

lines at seminars and workshops to ask you questions, holding the magazine that employs you or publishes your column in their hands. Sometimes they e-mail you and ask you to have lunch. They are often tan, fit, and from Florida. Rock groupies want to sleep with rock stars, and maybe leave their demo tape and hope the rocker puts in a good word for them. Journalism-grad girls are mainly interested in the latter two elements.

"How do I break into magazines?" they ask with pouty lips (at times that includes guys). "How can I become a magazine writer?"*

You take them to lunch, because they're pretty and they're smiling at you, and you think that somebody might have also taken you to lunch at some point and it's good to give back.

---

*In case you're interested in the responses, most compassionate magazine editors who judge a low possibility or need of seducing the J-school grad questioning them will answer these two questions with an honesty that will hopefully keep evolving in their career, but in large part contains these five points:

1. I don't know how you get into magazines. Asking a magazine person how you get into magazines is like asking a surfer how you make a wave. Try to be there when it comes, with your trunks and a surfboard. And take notes and write for free as long as necessary while surfing.

2. Don't approach any magazine unless you're willing and able to produce an exact duplicate of the stuff they run, without any of your own flair or talent or twist or creativity. An exact duplicate. Figure out if you'd be willing to do that, and reverse-engineer an article to see if you're currently able to do that without wishing you had never asked or concluding that varmint taxidermy would be far more enjoyable.

3. Don't buy or read any more "how to get published in magazines" books. The good ones you already have are plenty worthless enough.

4. Start with microscopically small, news-based items. They get killed and need filling every month, unlike the 4,800-word piece you're pitching on your hair stylist's colitis.

5. If you have extreme talent and chutzpah and a winning way, ignore all this, write your own rules and hire me in a decade or so, since magazine publishing tends to put a bullet in your head around the time you turn forty-four. Look at any magazine masthead from 1987 and try to find those people now.

You like the attention.

You help them. You give them a name. You refer them to another editor. You wax authoritatively about an industry you've apparently conquered and a world you've apparently turned into your personal marionette, not mentioning that you hope you aren't replaced by a bulletin board or a Magic 8 Ball next week.

Take the J-school groupies and the placating hopefuls and hucksters who are angling to get themselves or their products publicity, mix in a lot of youth, and it's easy to see why magazine publishing is rife with young men who fancy themselves as celebrities and who work their connections to bed models, soap opera actresses, and the arbitrary tail they encounter in the couch rooms of Soho lounges.

I dipped into this world and was graciously vomited from its inner circle.

That was due to my un-losable squareness and the quiet unease I somehow molecularly give to others who want to enjoy themselves in ways I've never mastered. I'm no good at cocaine. I don't like (don't like, don't like) cocaine, since I cannot help but associate it with self-congratulatory eigthies finance guys and spoiled starlets, all of whom need a good ass beating. I have nothing against the substance of cocaine itself, which is blameless because it's an inanimate substance. I think if these types of people had somehow connected themselves reputationally with oatmeal cookies, I would look with derisïon upon Mrs. Fields. And if I got into blow, I observed, I might have to start enthusiastically hugging other guys I barely knew instead of shaking their hand, or looking at others with the smirk of an insider joke and making an almost inaudible pig snort to cue that it was time to call "Quimby the pharmacist," and play other parts that would make me look like a bad summer-stock actor. Pot smoking grown men? Who are not professional musicians? I think if I had come home and seen my father opening windows and spraying Glade with a shit-eating grin on his face, I might feel differently about a dude lighting up a doobie after high school and frat houses were behind him. But I never did, so I find it weird. Ecstacy, another fave of the very early millennium, was too touchy-feely for me. The people I know who liked the now un-vogue Ecstasy were people who felt strongly about pandas and always wore brown suede sneakers and T-shirts with snarky,* ironic, so-yesterday-it's-way-ahead-of-you, would-not-be-cool-except-I-know-it's-not-cool-and-we're-in-New-York types of slogans or utterances on them. Such as "I loves me mac-n'-cheese." The less sense these words make, the stupider and less hip you are for not understanding this level of understated devil-nay-care brilliance.

Trusty alcohol, thank God, I can get behind. It ruins lives from Yale to jail, as AA says, so it doesn't have any preferen-

---

*This word is used often among magazine publishing types. It's an adjective that means attitudinal and sarcastic, even slightly caustic and belligerent with an overall purpose to convey smugness in the security that you are smarter or more informed than the person you're ridiculing, often in the earshot of a group you're hoping to make laugh at the expense of the person. Snarkiness is often an effective smoke screen when you don't know an answer, or realize you don't know something embarrassingly important or core to who you represent yourself to be, as snarkiness discourages challengers by conveying a denigrating cynicism that insinuates the issue is either (1) too simple and self-evident to bother explaining or (2) so far beneath your concerns that it's better left for idiots to chew on. Snarky people now frequently expose snarkiness, upping the ante.

tial or monopolistic tainting from one particular group to make me snobbishly dislike it. Luckily, the lowbrow clique in magazine publishing enjoys a great deal of alcohol, as does everyone in Manhattan . . . dare I say even more so than in Allentown (no car keys in your pocket to guilt you into not having that eleventh beer). This lovely common denominator made my time among the young, snarky, twenty- and early thirty-something magaziner crowd enjoyable and, at times, fruitful for the dating column, since the women in this compete-for-airtime environment are almost always funny and smart, outgoing and up for anything. If her snarkiness isn't overboard, the rare woman in this circle can even tease you into thinking she might be that transformational Virgin Mary[*] you've been searching for.

That's the snarky magazine clique comprised of guys who wear slogan T-shirts. Another magazine clique, the one in pressed Armani suits, hangs out in places like Michael's restaurant and Elaine's bar.

I was vomited from this clique more quickly.

2.

Elaine's on the Upper East Side is one of the standard journalistic and literati hangouts, a place where book writers and playwrights (why isn't it *playwrites?*), mag and newspaper fixtures elbow with celebrities, theater stars, and local govern-

---

[*]Except she's slept with two to four guys in the immediate magazine clique and everyone openly jokes about it.

ment pols. At the afterthought of a bar, hopeful, tight-dressed, gold-digging dames and forlorn guys in suits mill together, wondering what happened to their life, hoping that maybe tonight they'll have finally legitimized their status through osmosis and steady patronage, and that tonight, just maybe tonight, they'll finally catch the eye of a big shot shuffling past them from the entrance, or sitting wistfully at one of the front tables.

The bright lighting, frequent seat changing, and six-hour sandbagging by patrons who all know or recognize each other, happily or not, makes Elaine's feel more like a sprawling, communal kitchen table rather than a bar or a restaurant.

It's been sitting on Eighty-eighth Street since the early 1960s, when Elaine bought the place and made it a friendly refuge for people scraping along in the writing biz, as long as they understood that she was in the restaurant biz when they occasionally had a couple bucks in their pocket.

"What's the difference between then and now? Now it's all kids!" Elaine said to me with an upturned palm on the table in her hushed, exasperated, that's-a-dumb-question-here's-your-answer-think-of-something-better-to-say-to-me-if-you're-gonna-talk-at-all-for-chrissakes tone, which she dialed up to warm and jibing with people she loved, dialed down to "*What?!*" with people she distinctly didn't, and delivered exactly as stated above to the steady stream of well-meaning newcomers and repeat-visit-guest-strangers like me, who wavered at the bottom of her affection scale but might be climbers if they spent a little more time or money there (the restaurant biz ain't making it on small talk over appetizers). And got less stupid with their questions.

I was invited to Elaine's a handful of times as a vouched-for guest of the new editor of *Men's Health,* who, like other media guys in their thirties, had become a regular patron there.

"You used to have to work for years to get a book or a big job, but now with television and newspapers, they're all— *hey!"* Elaine yelled in the direction of the bar.

"If your father saw you now he'd be ashamed of you! *Ashamed!"* She screamed at an early thirtysomething girl in a whorey dress and high heels, though her scream was hardly ever a raised voice, only a rise in emphasis. "I don't want to see you here like that. He'd be ashamed!"

The woman smiled at Elaine, trying to dismiss the harpoon with an "I'm all grown up now" smirk, but it melted into a face that could not hide its hurt. She turned back to the bar, not pretty now, when she had been six seconds before.

Elaine didn't know you well until the moment she showed that she did. She knew all about you, and all the yous before you first walked in here and the yous that'll come after you're gone or forgotten.

"They're all younger now?" I said to her, hoping she'd finish her thought.

"What?!" she said.

I thought about mentioning that all those literary types and newspaper dicks might have just seemed older to her forty years ago, since she was hosting them from the vantage point of a woman in her teens and twenties, but decided this would probably not be received well. And, of course, I believed she was correct, at least in regard to the people at her bar. As in all industries with the possible exceptions of Benedictine monkhood and fine tailoring, the Internet era, middle-class stock-trading explosion, an overall rising standard of living (not to mention the extended reach of capital offered by credit cards, examples of reality-show flunkies getting six-figure book deals, and the greater youth-centric focus in TV and in magazines such as *Maxim* and *FHM*), has almost assuredly crammed most of the non-pittance-paying jobs in media full of bucks who are far younger than the people who occupied those spots decades ago. Though it's hard to find someone who'll admit this who doesn't have an agenda or seething anger about being rendered obsolete.

I contemplated commiserating with Elaine and saying, "Damned brat-ass kids," but decided this also would probably not be received well.

3.

"Ladies, he's an eligible bachelor and he writes a dating column in a magazine!" one of Elaine's most esteemed white-haired stewards announced one Wednesday night, laying his fingertips on my shoulders after placing me at one of the coveted front tables, showing that my aura of vouchness from the *Men's Health* editor the week before still lingered, if briefly.

The eyes of four women studied me, scrutinized me. They showed me their white teeth.

"Is that true?" one chided the maître'd before turning to me. "Is that true? What are your dating secrets?"

"His introductions," I pointed.

"You're a dating expert?" said a late twentysomething, retro-bespectacled MTV exec at the table with a too-made-up woman clinging to him. "Really, come on, tell me some of your secrets."

My secrets.

I'm a five-foot-six guy with thinning hair and I was writing a dating column, so his question had a practical ring to it, as if it expected something more substantive than, "Well, when you got it . . ."

"I assure you I have no secrets," I said awkwardly. As much as I tried, as much I enjoyed watching this quiet carnival of young and old figures posturing for recognition and sighing with the fatigue of having postured for too many years, engaging in animated conversations and looking on silently while longing, at least for tonight, for the warmth of genuine reconnecting . . . I was about as comfortable in this world as Andy Sipowicz sitting in a hot tub with Ryan Seacrest.

4.

A few minutes after being seated, I watched the staffer who introduced me to these lovely people accept another hug from a patron that was the standard-issue mogul-ish "my man" hug I had given him ten minutes earlier. This was a full-body, long-lost-relative, you-just-pulled-my-baby-out-of-a-burning-car hug that included two squeezes and two backslaps. Aside from me and the new entrant, he received this hug from almost all of the seeming regulars who came to Elaine's, including all the usual journalistic characters and stage and screen boldfaced names, and ex-principles from *Falcon Crest* (females just added a cheek kiss to the above embrace). It was a beautiful kind of hug. Any more emotion would require cradling faces with open palms and biting one's upper lip at a loss for words. Which may be added to the greeting next year.

After several years of sincere hugs and being like family to these cologned and well-shod guests, deciding who would get the warmest welcomes or front tables as their wattage flared and dimmed, handing slips of paper with destination tips and insider-info scribbles, he ran afoul of his employer over a small squabble and was asked to consider leaving, or decided to leave, or a combination of both.

I ran into him at a bar far downtown, alone. He was broke, eating on the arm of the friendly bartender, a loyal pal of his and a kindred spirit to the vagaries of the bar business. Surely, at least a few of Elaine's clientele had called him, or invited him to call, or had offered to make a call on his behalf.

Surely.

He laughed and dug into his chicken pot pie.

5.

On my last visit to Elaine's, my vouchness long evaporated and my proper anonymity restored, I watched the matriarch of the saloon accept her guests while carefully watching her workers operate. She took a kiss from Burt Young, a kiss and hug from Dan Aykroyd, and invited a scraggly bearded Christopher Walken to sternly sit with her. At least from an outside observer's view, I noted that night, she's living the perfect bachelor's life. If the woman I'm hoping to find doesn't show up, if the kids don't materialize, if I never have those things to be my predilection, maybe there is an alternative to being alone. Namely, never being alone. Having a saloon full of hundreds of surrogate lovers, old and new, many you trust, others you don't, many you like, others you don't, many you don't even know and don't need to. A regular cache of people, there every night you are, insulating yourself against loneliness. Against the very thought of loneliness.

Elaine is not a young woman, and her girth has caused some to comment, with admiration or fear or both, as to how she persists. But persist she does. Watching absently from my far table, I found myself tastelessly wondering just how many of these sons of bitches would be there to put a rose on her casket if they heard no one else was showing up.

CHAPTER SEVEN

A Reporter Gets His Comeuppance

1.

"What are you going to do if you meet someone? What if she wants you to stop writing the column?"

This was a common curiosity. I shared it. Sometimes it came in from e-mails, other times from the regulars in my local on Fifty-fifth Street, Matt's Grill, who thought the columns were either gems or trash, usually depending on their sex. And sometimes it came from the editors at *Men's Health* and other magazines who wondered if the crap I was chronicling was true.

"I'm contractually forbidden from settling down," I'd often reply, which made a handy first date comment if I had any reason to suspect that I might have another potential Carla staring at me from across the table.

"The column will then be renamed to 'This Dating on the

Side Life,'" I said other times, though no one ever found this funny.

"I'll cross that blessed bridge when I come to it," I told others who actually wanted an answer, occasionally adding that dating without the hope of finding someone isn't dating, it's dallying. Some men dally. Some women dally. It doesn't have the stakes or the emotion or investment of dating, at least for the dallying party, because they're shopping for gifts they know that they'll never give anyone. Dallying isn't looking, it's deciding to find at will because what's found doesn't matter. Unlike my earlier dive into Match.com, I was now dating. Getting into a constrictive relationship was the point.

"Do women know you're writing this column? Do you tell them you're going to write about them?"

This question always came second if it didn't come first.

And it came only from people who were not at all familiar with modern dating.

My usual answers were "usually" and "usually," though "are you kidding?" became a far more honest response about eight months into the column's life. Trying to hide it was futile.

Within a time span of ten seconds to two days after learning my last name, any woman I had asked out after meeting her online or anywhere else had read every column I had written so far. Upon the first date they knew about my disgruntlement with Mimi's insistence on always being completely naked, all the time, whether we were being sexual or not. They knew about Amy's thong. They knew about my adventure of having two back-to-back guests in one weekend nearly collide due to my poor scheduling skills complicated by a stab at stunning pomposity.

This was due to a neat dating innovation called Googling.

A few times, they called and canceled a date after Googling me.

"I don't want to be objectified for your commercial gain," Athena sniffed at me.

"How do you know if you haven't tried it?" I asked her.

Most times they said nothing whatsoever, and did not admit they that had Googled me until the end of the first date or, if it was in the cards, the middle of the second date.

"I admit it, I read your columns online and found the current issue," several said. "Don't worry, I won't get naked tonight."

2.

One Saturday morning at 7:40 A.M., the phone rang with a vicious portent. It was Amy. And she was vicious.

"Bastard!" she screamed.

Not fully awake, I ran through the files in my mind frantically trying to identify which transgression she was most likely talking about.

"You are never going to know what's it like to find someone," she spat at me. "You are always going to be alone."

I needed coffee.

3.

I had written about one of our previous dates. The one in which we went for a summer walk, had dinner at Patsy's, and then caught a nightclub show at the Carnegie Club of a guy singing Sinatra tunes.

That night, I felt closer to her than I ever had. She was looking at me with Alice eyes, and laying with her, even though our canoodling was limited by her menses situation, I felt a deep happiness that for me (maybe especially for me) was more—or more accurately, differently—satisfying than any in-and-out sex summit I had enjoyed with any woman.

I'm sure that it was for this precise reason that I had to write about it and make sure a mushroom cloud would be over the whole deal in a matter of weeks.

She brought to my attention that my reporting of the details of our date included startling inaccuracies.

"Green dress? You said I wore a green dress! Who wears a green dress? It was a black dress!"

"Of course I remembered that it was a black dress, Amy," the radio therapist lied. Naturally I did not remember that. What she didn't understand is that I remembered everything pertinent about her from that evening, such as how her skin felt on my face, the scent of her neck, the melody of her voice. Her sighing in the next room as she looked in her bag, and me buttoning my shirt and hearing her sigh, and loving the twoness that sigh meant. We were both there, separately, tending to our own small thing without a single thought about what the other was doing, what they were thinking, if we were on solid ground or anything at all, and at that instant I thought this is why you put up with everything. I had dated women for months, girlfriends who had become far more ensconced in my life than Amy, without ever feeling that small sensation.

The color of her dress must have seemed as important to me as the parsley on a plate.

4.

In listening to her rant, it did dawn on me that everything about her I did remember was comprised of only those things that meant something to me. Which the blackness or greenness of her dress did not. That perhaps this was something significant to her, or why, I couldn't venture to say.

"I changed the color of your dress to green so that it would be one of those details just between us, Amy. I wanted to keep some things private. . . ."

She wasn't buying it.

"And then the mammaries," she cried. "Did you have to use the word *mammaries?*"

". . . It felt like the right word," I said.

Her mammaries *had* spilled forth from her strapless black dress as we walked down the street, so powerless was it to contain her ample Zancoskies, and, as I wrote, I *had* wished that I had been carrying a bullhorn and gun to fend off the rabid, hungry stares of men who meant her no good and who were not me.

We had so many misunderstandings to clear up.

Within twenty minutes, she was civil, and I was reaching for the Advil.

"It was a beautiful night, Amy, I hope—"

"It was our night, Ron. I wanted to keep it for us. I asked you not to write about it, and you said you wouldn't."

"I'm sorry I wrote about it."

"I'm afraid for you, I'm afraid that you're never going to know what it's like to find someone," she repeated.

This prophecy nicked my aorta. She knew me well enough to know what to say.

"Amy, if you came to New York, I could fall for you," I said minutes later.

This may have been my heartfelt version of proposing. At least proposing an invitation to a relationship that might lead to pre-engagement seriousness.

5.

One week after our explosive Saturday morning call, we spoke again. Her silence that week had been telltale, and she told me what I suspected was coming.

"I've . . . met somebody else," she said. "Someone I knew from Toledo. I'm going back. I think I'm going to be happy with him."

I'll never know if this other chap's fitness to be Amy's Toledo sweetheart was enhanced by my relative neglect of her in those weeks, not to mention the green-dress felony. But I know where I'd bet the smart cash.

The radio therapist told her this other man was lucky.

After hanging up with her, he soothed me, and pointed out a lone bright side.

"I guess we have a topic for the next column, don't we?"

CHAPTER EIGHT

I See Single People

1.

Reeling from Amy's blow, alone, frustrated from a spell of nine less than fruitful encounters with women I met online, and worrying about keeping a stream of steady content coming for the column, I hit the singles circuit in Manhattan. I attended every cocktail hour, roof garden party, speed dating event, museum outing, hike, movie-and-wine/beer night, and cooking class I could reasonably fit into a week. I only drew the line at scavenger hunts and events that seemed like they would require name tags.

Due to my wide experience (if not conclusive success) with online dating Web sites, I also began writing an advice column on Match.com (called "Tell it to Ron," which the radio therapist loved), and teaching two-hour online dating seminars at the 92nd Street Y, an institution on the Upper East Side that offers classes, lectures, and events of A-to-Z variety, many of which, but not all, had a Jewish slant. While I had been around the e-block with Match.com, Matchmaker. com, and other general-population dating sites, many of the seminar attendees asked about J-Date, which was an online dating site for Jewish people and people who want to date them . . . more than a few of which, I would later learn, were not Jewish themselves.

"I like the quality of talent on there," a gentile man would say. "I'm just looking for a nice Jewish guy," a gentile woman would say. I found myself ruminating about the potential ethical grayness of their ambitions, always translating it into other races, ethnicities, and persuasions. What if a white Protestant woman says, "I'm just looking for a nice Pakistani dude?" What about a black guy concentrating his online dating searches on a site for Chinese people (and people who want to date Chinese people, in completing the parallel)? Or a WASP man who only wanted to date an Aboriginal Australian? Or a wheelchair-bound woman who only wanted to marry a midget? On and on I would mentally mix and match, constantly arriving at the same fundamental Seinfeldian truism that there was, inherently, nothing wrong with that. Except that, of course, in many of the pairings, there was something wrong with that. Perhaps there was just the faintest peep of potential wrongness. Usually it was due to the stereotyped notions of why an X would want a Y begging to be considered. I can hear Randy Cohen, the "Ethicist" columnist from the *New York Times*, saying something like, "Perhaps the heart wants what it wants, but the ethicality of this certainly depends on why . . ."

If only I could find that beautiful woman who, at this very

moment, is telling someone "Maybe I'm totally screwed up, but I just want to meet a five-foot-six guy who's infatuated with Sandy Koufax and old-time radio shows and is fearful of penetration. Is that too much to ask?"

2.

Most of the seminar attendees—as well as the singles I met in the other functions—were men and women in their thirties to fifties, many of whom had been divorced in the last three to ten years. I got to peek a little further down the road from my own peer group by working as a "host" at a variety of drink-and-hors d'oeuvres singles events billed for people aged thirty-five to forty-nine—which always turned out a crowd aged forty-three to sixty-four or thereabouts. My job was to wear a conspicuous "host" button and to chat up wallflowers, make the awkward mill-abouts feel better about dropping the twenty-dollar door fee to come to this rented bar from 8 to 11 P.M., and start conversations between men and women who otherwise would not interact—usually by choice.

This was what I was supposed to do.

Instead I usually got drunk and had a good internal cry.

It was a wrenching scene. I wasn't just looking at a group of unattached middle-agers (even the thirty-three-year-olds had a middle-aged air about them, probably from osmosis). I was looking at two hundred ghosts of Christmas (and Easter, and Mother's Day, Columbus Day, MLK Day . . .) Future. The typical apparition was a bald or badly toupee'd man with a paunch and a sour puss, twirling his Collins glass and eyeing each passerby and no one in particular, his dour regard radiating equal parts desperation and resentment. The look on his face was a droll sphinx of contradictions, a quiet plea that only makes a lick of sense to others who have worn the same visage: "You *could* talk to me even though I know you aren't going to, and believe me that's no skin off my ass. But I'm here."

At least no toupee yet, I would console myself, tugging at my scalp grass.

3.

The ominous thought that it may already be too late, and I may already be a loser, challenged my usual outlook on a matrimonial timetable that says I have infinite time. My father didn't marry my mother until he was thirty-nine (when she was still a teen). His life has always been the template on which I've based my own, for no other rationale than it seemed to work for him and its retarded agenda gives me a reassuring bounty of time. (If he had waited until his late sixties to get married, perhaps I'd only be heading off to college about now.)

Following his road map, I figured that I'd merrily enjoy myself until around age thirty-nine (as I've always supposed he did from 1915 to 1954, without any facts or information to verify or disprove this), and then, right on the cusp of turning forty, some cosmic switch would be flicked by God's finger and I'd meet a beautiful nineteen-year-old girl waiting tables in some Italian restaurant. She, of course, had been put there for the sole reason of saving me from becoming a dirty-pantsed indigent who would be institutionalized or, at best, end up being a punch line on a bar stool, serving as an advertisement for the necessity of marriage. We'd marry and get pregnant, or vice versa, and then, about fifty years later, I'd die.

Simple enough.

Having the foreknowledge of this agenda allowed me to tell several eligible and willing women to go bother someone else, either outright or by neglect, after dating them for a few weeks or months or on and off for longer periods. Good grief, I would think, when I'm forty, she'll be *forty*. What the hell am I going to do with an old cow like that? By the time I'm sixty-five, I'd be married to a geriatric. She'll barely have the strength to diaper me.

It seemed only a foreshadow of my own birthright that my father had a life studded with extraordinary luck, in which even the bad turns usually resulted in the best possible outcome. For a few examples, he was relocated from a village in Sicily to America in the Roaring Twenties, he escaped the sting of the Depression through steady barber work, he then escaped a short, bad marriage in his early twenties without the entanglement of children, he was drafted four times in World War II but given a 4-F pass for flatfeet each time, he was his own boss—if a relatively flawed one—for his last eighteen working years, he saw his house burned to a char while everyone was conveniently not home (even the two cats made it), he had a heart condition that never required a chest spreader, he never had any surgical invasion of his body until receiving a pacemaker at age eighty-one, he likely willed his own death on Christmas to steal some of Christ's waning yearly thunder, etc., etc. The nineteen-year-old girl popping into his life was just another good thing, albeit one of the huge good things, that had been routinely destined by whatever saint was in charge of lining up good things for Samuel.

If that saint had a son, surely I was on his assignment board.

4.

Watching these unpaired men and women mill around the single events fueled a chilling suspicion that my foolproof plan might only be proof that I was a fool. Life did not seem to have offered any circus safety net to these forsaken souls. They were not only living evidence that the worst can happen, but that it happens fairly frequently to people who have all four limbs and at least one good suit. I had never given a lot of thought about what alternative fates might be in store for me if my expectations didn't pan out, but now I had 437 examples crammed into the same bar.

In deference to Murphy's Law, and my ripening social hypochondria, I began viewing the likelihood that I'd join the cast of *The People That Life Forgot* as a sure thing. I had already passed several auditions, I realized. I was thirty-two and had never come close to marrying a woman. I owned no property. I had a freezer full of single frozen dinners, half a towel set that read *His*, and enough money saved to have a shot at financing a meager retirement for one. My favorite *Star Wars* character was Han Solo. The only card game I ever had any success in as a kid was Uno. My programmed existence was a binary one, a long repeating series of me's and nobodies, only interrupted by the sporadic If-Then sub-loop of occasional partners.

Without the two comped drinks, playing greeter at these singles parties might have been a total bummer.

5.

These singles shindigs were brimming with social research rewards, however. After attending dozens of them, I made some valuable scientific observations that I will record here for posterity. The interesting creature that I termed Homo Singulus—namely the thirty-five-plus-aged biped who has ceased thinking it will find a mate through serendipity and has "taken the bull by the horns" to make this goal happen—has five characteristics.

1. *They flock in groups and know all the dirt on each other.* The same single people repeatedly show up to the same events and, with little exception, spend their time talking to the same people. They all know each other's story.

"That's Charlie," a woman will tell you offhandedly. "I see he's having success with Jane tonight. I went home with him once and he's a total jerk. But Jane is desperate since her divorce so I worry for her."

"Sheila, Terry, Sue, and that fat quiet woman always come and talk to themselves, though occasionally somebody tries to pick up Sheila—her husband was a nine-eleven victim."

"Harry's rich and thinks you ought to be impressed with him and his boat-charter business, overlooking the fact that he's two hundred pounds overweight and a slobbering drunk."

"Jan's a dick tease. Just warning you."

And so forth.

Then there are the singles everyone knows by appearance, but who rarely speak to anyone. They show up at every function. I began mentally referring to them as Cliffies, Blanches, and Miss Havishams. One archetype, a very pretty blonde in her fifties, with a fit, sexy body, always wore the same strapless black dress with the same black stockings and the same nice pair of "night on the town" heels. She always looked expectantly at the crowd while she stood near the entrance with her something-and-soda, for upwards of three hours. She never danced, or spoke with anyone except in short bites to beg off or discourage a long conversation.

"Hello," I said to her, my host pin bigger than a coffee can lid. "I'm Ron. Are you enjoying the event?"

"Hi, I'm Ellen. Yes, I am. I'm just . . . I'm sorry, I'm waiting for someone."

Aren't we all.

"Some people don't want to be talked to, and will run from any interaction and there's absolutely nothing you can do to break through to them, so just leave them alone," the event's organizer lectured before each new event. Their twenty bucks is as good as anyone's, though, and they showed up reliably, so they remained on the list.

At times, in watching the familiar try to chat up the familiar with the same "well, uh, nice to see you" outcomes, I would get the gripping urge to overtake the DJ's station (who only played seventies songs—"Stayin' Alive," "Double Dutch," "Knock on Wood," and the like—underscoring that these peoples' lives had effectively ended in 1979), kick off the music, wrestle the mike away and deliver a much-needed public service announcement:

"Attention, *fools:* You have come to the same event and are talking to the *same people* for at least the tenth time in the last three months. It is *not* working for you. It will *not* work tonight. It will *not* work next week, when you spend another *twenty bucks* to talk to the *same* people at this or another 'upscale singles event for people twenty-eight to forty-nine.' And speaking of that, no one is being a prick about enforcing that forty-nine thing, but *good god*—if you're not even a *decade* close to that, why do you think they even bother to list an age limit? What will it take to insult you? Yes, *you!* As I said, you are *not* going to *find someone*—which you all claim is your goal—if you keep engaging in the *same behavior* that has resulted in *failure, again* and *again* and *again.* This is the very definition of *insanity. Stop being insane.* Filter out. Take a pottery class. Join the Sierra Club. Go to a *new bar* and waste twenty bucks there. *Do something else. Anything else.* Thank you."

2. *Several of these singles are not simply nice people hoping to find another nice person to love, but are mentally troubled, angry, or imbalanced individuals who should be shunned.* Social retardation is merely one of their symptoms. This was usually so obvious, I made these diagnoses all by myself without the hindrance of training.

One short, thirtyish woman with bobbed, light hair was looking a little hesitantly at the sea of single humanity in front of her as she stood near the restrooms, so I approached her, my host button glowing like the moon.

"Hi. Are you enjoying the event?"

She looked up at me with terrified eyes and took a big step back. There was now four feet between us, so I inched closer to be within earshot.

"I'm Ron. I can get you a drin—"

"No." Another step back.

I looked at her. She looked at me. I inched forward, intrigued.

"What's your name?"

Another step back.

"Claire. Please—" She put her hands up, palms facing me.

I instinctively talked to her like she had a gun pointed at a child's head.

"I swear to God, I won't come any closer. Just calm down. I just wanted to see if you want a drink."

"I'm just—please," she said, hands raised, her chin trembling.

I had the urgent temptation to leap forward and give her a crushing bear hug, burying her face in my shirt front while screaming "That's my baby!" I regret chickening out, since opportunities like that are rare. It either would have killed her or been the excruciatingly cathartic breakthrough she needed, like the one in the end of *Good Will Hunting*. More likely it would've killed her.

Since this was the only time a woman reacted to me this way, at least without knowing me, I assumed she had the problem. Though another occurrence will signal a trend.

While Claire had an extreme example of paranoia, or at least guyaphobia, others spanned the dial. You'd spot healthy self-esteem about as often as garden faeries.

3. *Most of the never-marrieds have unrealistic expectations and standards regarding romance.* (Duh, indeed.) Most female homo singuluses are looking for their soul mate—the guy who will look past their unattractiveness, or their weight problem, or their conversation-hogging, or their woe-is-me-ism, or their constant clinging and need for assurances, or their long-compiled philosophies and commandments concerning relationships ("We do not settle," one woman said to me with a finger wag), or their compulsive debt accumulation, or their chronic skittishness or cat hoarding. Such a thing as a soul mate—or at least what they're imagining—only exists in bad movies usually made by women for women. And the guys who are willing to overlook these things, they find, are either use-her-and-lose-her jerks, or, far worse, riddled with similar flaws that these women are definitely not willing to overlook.

Many of these never-married women also use online dating Web sites, which aggravates their futile and endless soul mate quest, as I've already mentioned. With hundreds of possible men to choose from online, and another single event coming in three days which, this time, just might cough up Mr. SM (instead of Mr. S and M), it's easy for these women to remain in perpetual hunt mode. Often a group of three or four girlfriends will reinforce this belief in each other. And talking about the flunkies who were definitely not Mr. SM is good fun.

Many of the never-married men, on the other side of the bar, want young honeys. (Duh again.) They're still shooting for their own version of a soul mate, who typically wears a size 4. Since they've never come close to snagging such a dish (many of these guys are geeks and misfits of a breathtaking degree), but they do get willingly rolled for free dinners by young beauties now and again, they figure it's as likely to happen now as ever. The women who aren't openly repulsed by them (who are numerous) are highly wary due to the "he's forty-six and has never been in a serious relationship" warning bell.

4. *The divorced homo singuluses are not looking for each other.* Experience has made them more realistic, though many still have the above aspirations. Talk to the men (as I found in my own ad hoc focus groups), and you'll find out they want to get married again, and most do not expect the chick to be perfect or twenty-three years old. Most don't want her to be perfect or twenty-three, even though it's a fun daydream. ("What am I gonna talk to her about?")

He doesn't give a damn if she's been married or not, or what she does for a living; she's just got to be non-harsh on the eyes and warm and not a carping bitch. The men who say, "I'll never get married again" want a life with all of the benefits of marriage that strangely sounds a lot like marriage, since forty-plus men who live without a woman for long stretches of time tend to destroy themselves. Typically, the divorced guy was booted from his marriage, rather than leaving on his own accord, so he's more angry or regretful than fed up with women or marriage for good.

Tragically, the women these guys are looking for aren't usually in these rented bars, circling the wood at a singles event. They're sitting in the Bennigan's across the street with their girlfriends, several of whom are married. These women are not looking for guys at singles functions. They're scared of them.

The divorced women at these events want a guy who's not going to fall apart on them, and who is not as big of a loser or control freak or philanderer as the last ass they married. And he's gotta have money cause she's broke. But they scrutinize the living shit out of every divorced guy because, good grief, they found him cruising at a singles mixer and sipping his highball in a group of hellaciously undesirable men. And he was somebody else's headache. Men sense this scrutiny and don't much care for it. Their ex-wives were big on scrutinizing, and noticing every little spot where they came up lacking, and generally busting their balls. "They're all psychos here," some men will tell you.

Succinctly, many (not all—don't egg me on the street) of the never marrieds at these "upscale singles parties" are defective toys looking for the one person who will play nice with them regardless, and the divorced people are moths with one wing singed from a flame. They fear the incendiary.*

---

*The masochistic or savior types who have dated or married scores of bad eggs are easy to avoid at singles events, because they're not usually there. In my experience, most typically don't spend a lot of time trolling for new relationships; they take what comes when it comes, and spend a lot of time playing the role of toilet paper to their latest owner. People at singles events are usually inept exploiters. It's kind of like trying to find a criminal genius in prison.

5. *Singles are an extremely exploitable consumer group and easy, frequent victims of fraud.* Finding a mate becomes a heart-panging, life-or-death mission to many thirty-five-plus singles, one in which they see two outcomes: either they find a match, or they embark on a bleak future of loneliness and isolation in which they end up a wizened and withered corpse that's deposited in a potter's field. (I empathize.) Dropping twenty dollars on a bar mixer, forty dollars on a speed dating event, or two hundred and fifty dollars on an organized "12 men + 12 women" dinner outing every week is just the wee start of their outlay. You'll meet dozens who have shelled out thousands of dollars from their paltry savings to join "upscale" (marketers love that word) introduction services, and a large number have also had dalliances and near misses with matchmakers. Oh, Christ, matchmakers.

Chatting up the incidental person who's dropped ten thousand dollars, twenty thousand dollars or much more to work with a professional matchmaker (and is not a millionaire, nor even highly financially comfortable) is a humbling experience. Humbling in that you realize a fellow mammal like yourself could exhibit such stupidity, gullibility, or capacity for drastic measures due to desperation, and also humbling in realizing that if you had any smarts at all, you'd be a matchmaker. (Naturally, I only heard the war stories of matchmaker failures at singles events, as the successes were presumably home snuggling with their twenty-thousand-dollar honey. I'll hit my own bout with a matchmaker in Chapter 14.)

At organized singles functions, it's common for good-looking female reps from expensive introduction services to crash the party (posing as just another love seeker) and hand out cards or brochures to both men and women (they gain the men's confidence for obvious visual reasons, and women assume an attractive girl wouldn't waste her time on a service full of losers, so they'd be in good company). Usually the soiree organizers toss out these women as soon as they spot them, since they're often peddling competing services. Other times they're admitted with the blessing of a shared commission. In that case, two babe-a-licious women will sit at a booth, make eye contact with the timidly foraging homo singuluses who file by, and flirt brochures into lapel pockets. Into my lapel pockets, more than a handful of times.

I'm only human. These girls smell nice.

Type *singles* into Google and you'll see thousands of services angling for the single person's dollar. The vast majority of these businesses, in my vastly generalized and easily litigatable opinion, are not designed to get single people married. They're designed to sell single people products and services for as long a period a time as possible.

Why? It's a unique product these singles are buying, one in which the therapy of just trying it—having the courage and gumption to do something about your love life other than wait and pray—is part of the purchase.

Secondly, most singles will tolerate failure for long periods of time while still paying for the services, since they're accustomed to tolerating long periods of failure. A big boon to the exploiters in the singles industry: They're under no pressure to give their clients any guarantee of success—in fact, they cannot guarantee any degree of success unless they're engaging in a covert slave trade. And their most dedicated client base will, with rare exceptions, accept most of the damning responsibility for not snaring a new love (or at least failing so far . . . what good fortune might come their way next week?). They're accustomed to accepting rejection or a loveless life as their fault because (1) it usually is, since many are toads or painfully awkward; (2) it's been the long status quo of their lives; and (3) they've been told it's their fault on more than a handful of occasions.

The looming nuclear threat that these singles (meaning the subset of those homo singuluses who are willing to spend vast sums of money to find their mate) want to avoid being confronted with is the most painful subtext of their failure. Namely, this subtext is: "We haven't found you a match because you're fucking ugly, fat, strange, and overall nobody's idea of a catch."

They're pretty used to berating themselves with similar statements in their dark moments, and they've sought the help of an introduction service or a matchmaker to disprove—or at least repress—these painful suspicions, however obviously true they might be. (Again, I empathize.) The compassionate-sounding marketer can tickle their ugly/fat/strange vulnerability by overtly not going there. "The right person's out there, Maude/Melvin, so let's not get discouraged. We'll find them. You're too special to remain alone, and they're looking for you, too. Let's change our tack a bit and press onward. . . ."

Some singles have told me these stories at events and seminars, sometimes fishing for the opinion of a "famous-dating-columnist-I've-never-heard-of" on whether they should drop out of the service, or try this other introduction service that offers the same thing. Some wanted to know if I had met people who had a similar bad experience other than the few they've bumped into.

These singles are the willing consumers in a self-help industry that is, in some significant ways, just like the diet industry.

They feel excited about using the service at the start, and just knowing that they've made the investment makes them feel like they're giving their own lives a big kick in the quality department. And, importantly, the biggest repeat consumers assume that they fail repeatedly because, well, they're pigs.

One big difference, however, is that anyone can tell if a diet is either working or not working while they're testing it. Its effectiveness and potential for ultimate success (if that exists in the weight loss or relationship realms) can be gauged incrementally. But introduction or dating services or matchmakers, unlike marketers hawking a diet, can dangle the carrot (or cheese Danish) that the instant success and redemption and love and sex and a lonesome existence averted could come at any beautiful random cinematic moment—that moment when the service belches forth the forty-seventh candidate who is, finally, your soul mate or your wife-to-be. A Jenny Craig rep can't claim that you may see no results for a year and then suddenly wake up on a Tuesday morning looking like Giselle. But introduction services can insinuate precisely that. Frustration and futile parings may only be a prologue to your new life with that perfect person . . . if you'll just send another check, that is.

If it sounds like I'm incensed about the easy exploitation of

singles, I am. Not because I deeply care for these people in-
trinsically, if I must be honest, but mainly because they're
such easy marks. It's not like the hucksters and con artists are
fooling circuit court judges and getting the zoning approval to
build fake ATMs in shopping malls. They're sidling up to
broken toys and singed moths and saying, "You don't need to
be alone. I can help." People who shake money from singles
without the strong intentions to actually deliver them a mate,
and thus eliminate them as a customer, are *this* close to the
scum who offer dying cancer patients phony serums.

I'll get off my soap dispenser now.

Here's hoping the FTC will soon recognize singles as a distinct consumer group and put the hammer down on the
SOB's who fleece them.

And here's hoping I won't give a goddamn about this in
ten years.

CHAPTER NINE

You're Him?

1.

It had been a year and a half since I had moved to New York, and I had written fourteen columns. For the first time, I began staring at the blank screen and stifling the urge to retch.

"We need another one like 'The Old Flame,'" Tom, my top editor, said to me over a burger. He meant the piece about my dinner-date reunion with Nicole, the woman who had become a singular obsession of ridiculous proportions to me some years before. That piece was an accident. Something happened—namely, her recontacting me—which gave me a natural chance to recount something horrible and heartfelt and atrociously real.

"It's hard to make those happen," I laughed.

He read me. Tom wasn't just the editor of the column, he was a guide who regularly prevented me from looking like a huge boob in print. This is to say that Tom was a good editor.* Incidentally, most people have no clue what that really means, because they have no idea what editors do. They think you correct typos or take what writers send you and figure out where to put it in the magazine. Now, there's no reason people really should know or care what magazine editors do; it's not like I walk into the Gap and demand to know exactly how a T-shirt got from Sri Lanka to here before I buy it. But in the interest of being an honest ambassador I make the mistake of trying to give a semi-honest answer when asked:

"Editors come up with story ideas, or help refine an idea, and then we find a writer or negotiate with the one who

---

*There are good editors and bad editors. Tom was a good editor. It generally pays to be a mediocre editor. Bad editors tend to create tons of shit work for themselves by not telling the writer exactly what piece the magazine really wants, if they even know themselves. Good editors tend to get a lot of shit work because they're burdened with assigning challenging pieces to well-known writers, several of whom are egotistical frauds who are no longer willing to work. Mediocre editors, however, are just good enough to wring usable stuff out of mediocre writers, which is the stuff that fills magazines. In most economies, this makes replacing them just a little bit more of a pain in the ass than keeping them. By sticking with mediocre articles and mediocre writers, they avoid long, tortuous dances with problematic "high concept" pieces and with difficult name writers who are conceited bastards. Following the definition of mediocre, the majority of magazine editors are mediocre—but most ruin the experience because they don't think they're mediocre or they sincerely believe that receiving good-editor recognition and success is either long overdue, blocked by scheming saboteurs, or otherwise rightly theirs. For the mediocre editor to enjoy the optimal stress vs. effort sweet life, he or she must embrace being a mediocre editor and not be pissed off about their lack of excellence, or struggling against nature to be a good editor. That's hard, since a lack of ambition can get cancerous in people and whole staffs after a while. Bosses and writers usually tell editors, "You suck," or "You're brilliant," which can be true of the same editor in the same afternoon. But far more revealing feedback would be, "You are truly mediocre." Find an editor who responds to that with a sly Clark Kent wink, and you'll find a journeyman who will either be remembered fondly or not at all.

pitched the story, we tell them what the piece needs to accomplish to make it in the magazine, we bug the writer for the first draft if necessary, we send the first back draft with questions and requests and, in worst cases, sometimes pages of notes on what changes and additions are needed, then we might actually run their second or third draft with our changes, or send the second draft back with the same questions, or, worst case just under telling the editor in chief that we have nothing, we take their research and totally rewrite it ourselves so we can just get the damned thing into—"

By this time the questioner is either glazed or has moved as far as possible from me. A couple others may shoot back a somewhat incredulous follow-up in the vein of, "How do you get John Grisham to go through all that shit?"

I had attempted to consciously churn out a column that was just as raw and moving* as "the Old Flame" in the fall of 2001, and it taught me a lesson. Namely, I don't have the talent to fake deep feelings or fabricate profundity, at least not without producing a mash of embarrassing dreck that reads like a failed evangelist trying to convince you to join his Amway network.**

---

*By "raw and moving," I mean it was raw and moving compared to the rest of my dating columns, or anything else that I had ever tapped out of a keyboard with a metaphorical .45 pointed at my head. This is not to suggest that this ditty of an essay was genuinely raw and moving in the way something significant may be raw and moving, like *Schindler's List* or the *Cheers* finale. Imagine if your three-year-old made a crude drawing of you that, to your mild amazement, actually looked like you in small but distinct ways. Given that everything else he drew was Piaget-appropriate scribbles, you might say to your spouse, "This drawing Bennett just did is excellent." You'd be using *excellent* in the same way I'm using *raw and moving*.

**I fear that I've just written my own book review.

I supposed it helped that my Fall 2001 attempt at profundity was designed to be a fleck of mud in the wheel spokes of a bandwagon. Like one or two other writers at the time, I figured the terrorist attack on the World Trade Center might be worth writing about somehow. You want raw and moving? I'll break your frigging skull with raw and moving. I'll explicitly connect my bummer mood about dating and the loneliness of urban existence to an event that killed three thousand-some people and is uniformly considered to be such a raw and moving tragedy, any reluctance any reader has in being taken to a raw and moving emotional state by reading this piece will be, well, just the same as pissing on the graves of all those helpless people, who didn't even have graves.

The plan seemed sound.

I talked about seeing that sickening, dim egg-yolk glow over the smoldering cavity far downtown as I sullenly tried to console myself with a seventeen-dollar glass of wine in the Rainbow Room, where the view from the sixty-sixth floor would let me contemplate the city and also emptiness I called a dating life, while munching on Wheat Chex party mix and listening to a piano man tink his way sadly through "A New York State of Mind."

2.

"I think we should just put this in a drawer and do something else," Tom said at the time. "I have to say that . . . this is the first column you've done that just plain doesn't work."

I was shocked, furious, resentful, devastated, annoyed, and

then more grateful than could be conceivably expressed, all in the span of about ten seconds. It reaffirmed the writing lesson that is usually wise for me to follow when I can help it.

No art-making, jackass.

It also sent a chill through me, like the after-shudder of a near-death experience. I had written a bad column. *The column was fallible, and that meant it was killable.*

So? I countered.

You can't live without the income. And if you're not a dating writer, what the hell are you?

. . . An AARP editor? I offered.

There's a pickup line that'll make that nineteen-year-old princess wet her panties.

I had myself there.

3.

Angie was a lesbian, so maneuvering into a tryst with her that would allow me to talk about homosexuality in print (deep issue!) and, well, have a tryst with a lesbian, which seemed like a precious thing to do, even though I had done it in 1995 and was forced to assume that, in retrospect, it must have been much more fun than actual memory recorded. Why, I'm still not sure.

I rationalized that I had persuaded that girl from 1995 (Pat . . . not kidding, her name was Pat, but she was pretty) to cross the fence and apply her cunnilingual skills on my penis, which somehow seemed hot but made no sense. Perhaps it was the fact that I was with a girl who was having a sort of sex with a whole host of girls, which was, by some transitive property, akin to my having some sort of sex with a whole host of girls at once.

By this logic, though, every time I sleep with a woman I should experience something akin to sleeping with a whole host of men at once, and I'm pretty sure I don't.

Perhaps I thought I had captured a double agent who, with gentle questioning, would reveal intelligence that would change my life. "You're a woman so you know exactly how women think and what women want, but you also think like a man because you want women. You're an insider and a predator—must be nice, you greedy bitch! Now tell me what the frig to do! [Screaming and sound of sizzling electric shocks from salted wet sponge rigged to car battery.] Tell me!"

It dawned on me that the intelligence pried out of her lesbian vault might be of limited value. I envisioned her gasping, "All right, all right, first you find another lesbian who gets sick at the thought of dick. . . ."

I'm overthinking Angie, I said to myself. I've been programmed to be turned on by attractive lesbians ever since age nine, when I found a half-burned *Hustler* in the weeds down by Big Timber Creek, and I wasn't going to let the minutiae of whys and wherefores spoil that.

"Are you the famous dating columnist?" Angie said as we met for an early after-work drink at Matt's Grill.

Angie was a doll. Her blond hair arced around her face with light-brown tips that brushed her collarbones. I had met her online, as usual, and the lesbian thing came out on the second date. She slept with women off and on, but liked guys as well, and the babbling brook of online dating was a plentiful source of dates for her. She was technically bisexual, or tech-

nically a woman who liked men but took home a Cathy or a
Susan once in a while for variety, or vice versa with an occasional Carl or Steve.

She can be exaggerated up into a full-blown, full-time lesbian for purposes of concise storytelling and Tom Wolfe–type
reportage, I emphasized to my internal ethicist, who does not
like to be called a conscience because that nervous tyrant was
located in the huge office down the hall from him.

He silently pushed his glasses to the tip of his nose.

4.

I liked Angie, all ways around. The ten extra pounds Angie
was carrying were packed in perfect places. She was a meaty
Long Island girl. One who looked like she could hurl a
Coleman cooler full of beer onto a flatbed, yet also still wear
underthings that would vanish in a dryer.

She updated me on her fender bender, hooking us back to
our phone conversation of two nights before. Then, as usual,
we exchanged the logistics of siblings and where we fell in the
birth order. I watched her mouth, with those perfect teeth, as
if I were trying to memorize it for a long prison stint. I imagined all the women's tongues that have swiped those ivories.
Then one of the images included a crop-headed girl in a muscle shirt with a wad of Skoal dip in her mouth, smelling of a
greasy leather jacket, armpit hair sprouting from her like
crabgrass from a sidewalk crack. This momentarily revolted
me, though later I wondered why. Why would that image be
more sickening than one of her swapping oral juices with
much the same character, only with the addition of a penis?

The loose logic I arrived at was that I, as a man, couldn't relate to the urge to kiss a masculine lesbian in any way, and I couldn't animalistically understand Angie's desire to do so even though intellectually I knew it rang her bell. But her tonguing a trailer-trash dude in a wife beater at least made girl-boy sense. And if she was attracted to this man, who has eye-stinging body odor and blackened half teeth in my mind, then, hell, I could give her a fair facsimile of that in no time. Without steady beatings if that's what her little heart desired.

"I read your columns on the Internet, you should know," she said.

"Oh?" I replied. Here it comes, I thought. She's going to bitch about my objectifying women, or her not being interested in being with a guy who reveals so many private details every single month, or her already being disappointed at my seduction skills, since she probably knows a roomful of women who are more adept in getting into a girl's pants.

"Thanks for your interest," I said, jovially. "If you enjoyed them please write a letter to the magazine."

"They were very interesting," she only said.

"Hey, did you ever have the ricotta ravioli appetizer here?" she asked, abruptly changing the subject. I shook my head.

"Forget about it," she said, Long Island style, rolling her eyes to the ceiling. "It's good."

I glanced at the menu.

"Sounds good," I replied.

"Oh, it's *good*," she said, cocking her eye at me. I looked up. We locked stares for a full second.

I ordered two plates of ravioli.

Ten minutes later, we were swabbing vodka sauce off a

drum-cymbal–sized plate with chunks of bread. I was hoping she would bring up the *L* topic first, since she had spoken about it so freely in our last date. There didn't seem to be a seamless way to revive it. "Yes, well, that's interesting. But back to carpet munching, as we were discussing Tuesday. . . ."

Angie was into her third wine—which was in a stem glass so huge it may have been intended to house a bubbling filter, fish, and a skeleton at a sunken ship's wheel—and she was relaxing. Her elbows on the table, she folded her fingers into a platform and rested her chin, looking at me provocatively.

"Well?" she said.

"Well what?" I said, gently.

She cleared her throat and looked down at her legs. Nice legs, in a short skirt (it might have been green, might have been black, or scarlet . . . but her legs were nice).

"No brushing your knuckles against my bare thigh? What, don't I rate?"

I grinned nervously. I was more used to the kind of flirting in which I fished for something in a gesture or comment that was probably nothing. She was referencing one of my columns about a date with Amy, who had (sorry, Angie, don't wing a toaster at me) even nicer thighs.

"I don't do the same thing every time, for God's sake," I laughed.

"We'll see," she said, smiling quickly, then arching her eyebrows and mentronoming her head to a silent rhythm as if she was growing bored of waiting.

"Oh, Christ, here," I said, yeomanly rubbing two knuckle nubs at the seam of her green or scarlet skirt. "Is that nice? Now I can get out the checklist and tick that one off," I said.

She laughed in response and squeezed my business hand encouragingly, which I then removed.

5.

Twenty minutes later, I crammed into the restaurant's water closet and kicked up the toilet seat. Buzzed from the wine, I caught sight of my face in the black-spotted mirror five inches from my nose, my breath fogging it.

Well, what now, Hoss? I asked myself. I was on that rare date where one could, it seemed, plot a ready avenue of success. I had a marlin on the line and it wanted to be caught, if I was reading all of the signs correctly (which I rarely do). All I had to do was crank. Crank without screwing up the relatively simple act of cranking, knowing that a line break can happen at any split second if I do something stupid.

I remember every one of these "remember this cause it's good" time-outs, which is an out-of-body moment (a bathroom mirror helps) you snag in the midst of "just act don't think" joy, quickly reflecting that if life really is only about the journey, then you'd best dig out the camera and get a snapshot standing in this spot, here and now, because—to paraphrase a beer commercial—it might not get any better than this. And it doesn't, because most of the snapshots were taken with the beautiful naïveté of thinking you had made it into the secret garden and would dwell in there forever. That joy can't be bottled, but its taste is unforgettable. You flip through these snapshots when the mood necessitates it, sticking to those captured seconds and not any of the regrets that followed. Strange snapshots. Some clothed. Some in a basement that smells of beer and old wooden steps. Some are those perfect Iwo Jima moments when nothing could possibly ever be wrong again. If I had to die now and leave a million anticipated ecstasies on the table, visiting these snapshots might fool me into believing, if I tried hard, that I got my share out of the woman thing and ought to be grateful. Very grateful.

Even one snapshot might make me believe that. Jackie. Tracy. Jeanne.

Paul Simon ought to write a song about this.

6.

There was only one hitch.

I had the all-to-familiar feeling that she thought she was having ravioli with someone else. Namely, the guy in my column. The one who reeked of Plan B confidence and action. This is the impression women tend to get when they see six weeks of living distilled into nine hundred words. You have to leave out the parts about watching paint dry. Other women had exhibited a similar wordless disappointment when I showed up instead of "the dating guy."

"Why don't you take a woman out, treat her like gold on the first date, you know, be a gentleman, and then treat her like total shit on the second date?" an editor suggested to me. "You know, insult her, make her pay for her dinner. Then write about how she reacts. Guys always wonder if they'd do better if they were assholes."

"That's a fantastic idea," I had replied. "I'll see if I can find the right candidate." Experiments of deceit and abuse that involve other people are very easy to talk about, I thought.

"Whoa! You really strapped on the feed bag, bitch. No wonder you got an ass like Montana. Now how about giving me a hanji under the table here? I didn't come out just to listen to that dying cat voice you got."

I'm sure I would've pulled that off convincingly.

Yet that was exactly the bit of duality my dates were beginning to include. If I was going to be the guy on the page to every woman with Google access who consented to share alcohol with me and invite me into her studio apartment, I'd need to do more than live perpetually in my aforementioned cautionless Plan B mode. I'd have to become Cary Grant, only a shorter version with twenty extra pounds and rugged good looks that were more in line with Corky, the actor with Down Syndrome from *Life Goes On*.

I will not let them down, I resolved.

I kicked-flushed the toilet and returned to do my duty. I walked back to the table, seeing Angie's body, striking and groin tingling even at thirty yards in the dim light. She was beautiful, datable, sexy as a reformed southern streetwalker, and the lesbian thing was a nice bennie for whatever reason I gave credence to at the moment. But Angie was a three-month fling, at best. I could see that clearly. I knew in the first five minutes after meeting her that I could not envision lifting a white veil off her face. Maybe it was her Long Island accent. Maybe it was her bit on the phone about wanting to adopt a dozen foreign kids. Maybe it was the vision of me trying to keep a dying marriage together in three years, applying lipstick to my nipples while wearing a long blond wig and size thirty-eight teddy with garters.

Then again, maybe it was the way-too-forward proposition that she gave me a few minutes after our ravioli plates arrived: "If you treat me the way you treated Amy, I guarantee you'll have more fun."

That was a fairly odd gauntlet to throw down, from what she could have gathered in reading those few columns. Beating Amy, fun-wise, would be no easy feat from where I was judging things. If she was indeed built similarly to the standard human woman, the only way Angie could outdo Amy might be to pick up the tab and invite her last three female lovers to convene at her apartment when we arrived. I accepted her challenge.

7.

We went back to Angie's high-rise after dinner and began tousling on her bed.

"I'm sorry about the chest hair," I said. "I know it's probably not what you're used to anymore. Or I mean I hope you're not, unless some of those . . . women . . . I mean . . ."

"It's fine," she said, mocking me. "I'll vacuum later."

"Well, what do you think?" she asked after several minutes. She gestured to her completely naked body like a *Price Is Right* girl showing off a home juicer.

"Are you kidding?" I whispered. I kissed her torso softly. A wrapper was ripped and a prophylactic was unrolled, and this brief shift from the passionate to the clinical had the effect that it had at least five times before in three years, during first-time outings with a new partner, with its roots very likely embedded in my shameful phobia of intercourse.

Sensing an opportunity to humiliate me, my manhood ran for cover like a roach exposed to daylight.

Angie noticed within a half-minute and slowed the choreography. She maneuvered, stopped, maneuvered, then stopped and gave me the embarrassed look of mechanical trouble. I took a deep breath, held it, and methodically conjured every lesbian scene committed to film, which now seemed redundant. Then came those banned tapes from Amsterdam. Embellished memories of teen luck. Coeds gone jailhouse berserk. I spooled everything I had. Classics and B-reels that never failed. They failed.

"It's just . . . the wine," I said. "Wait a second."

"Wine'll get you every time," she said.

I tried to revive my string-cut puppet with concentration and grit. Jesus was summoned.

"Guess I'm no Amy," she said, laughing.

"Oh, no, don't be ridiculous," I said, still laboring. She smirked at me, as if to say, "Never wrote a magazine column about losing your wood, have you?"

One long, blistering minute later, I rolled off of her and covered my face with my hands, like a Mafia informant being shuttled to trial. She was with the dating guy. The one who exposed every detail of his love life for a living. And he was at the plate without a bat.

She rolled on her side and stroked my chest.

"It's okay," she said tenderly. "Orgasms are overrated."

I locked eyeballs with her, like Eastwood in *The Outlaw Josie Wales*. The stony crag of devastation was crumbling at my feet.

This was, as some say, zero hour. My own dignity, which was forfeitable in most negative circumstances, and also quite accustomed to being forfeited, wasn't the only dignity on the line. I wasn't alone in this bed. I was representing every man, every virile male creature, every Y-chromosomed glob of slime that had ever had its dignity challenged by an opposing female glob as not having even the lowly basic wherewithal to do the one lowly thing it was put on the earth to do. There was no way I was letting Angie go back to the Consortium of Lesbians and report at the podium that, indeed, those who were wavering in their decision to remain on the vulva diet should feel secure in their path, because she had scouted into the testicle camp and tested a general inhabitant, and even beneath being amusing, it ultimately lacked the basic wherewithal to do the one lowly thing it was put on the earth to do.

I saw the faces of five hundred million men, all looking at me in still hope like I was Neil Armstrong paralyzed by acrophobia on the ladder of the LEM. *I could easily do this for you, but I am not there*, they pleaded. *In the name of all the gods, damn you, proceed.*

This wasn't helping. I needed to make this personal.

I will become impotent, I transmitted down my spinal column. *One day I will be a sexless bag of wrinkled lard no longer able to please woman or self or small woodland creature.*

But not today.

Do not try me. If we fail now, I'll be a man with nothing left to lose.

Sensing the gravity of my threat, and having no clue as to how I might deliver on it, my penis took the initiative of self-preservation. For utterly no reason I could sense, in just the same way the evacuation had occurred, my staff returned slowly and deliberately.

You better thank God you did that, I transmitted.

I reared atop Angie like Popeye given spinach. I think I even heard the trumpet.

"Nice comeback," she said, minutes later.

"Had you going, eh?" I said, breathing up phlegm like I had just carried an oak dresser up three flights.

"I really enjoyed that trick, when you went in circles. Where'd you pick that up?"

"Yugoslavia," I said.

"I think you read it in *Men's Health.*"

"If you enjoyed it please write a letter," I gasped, praying that round two would offer no chance of humiliation or that sleep would come with haste. That one small step almost killed me.

8.

The next morning, Angie handed me a new razor over the shower curtain.

"I'm leaving you a new toothbrush on the sink," she said.

I fingered the curtain and peeped out. I saw her butt, under that short Chinese robe, exit.

I gotta get out of here, I thought. I rinsed rose-hips shampoo out of my hair and dried and dressed. This was supposed to be a three-month fling, but I needed to end it early. During the previous night's near-catastrophic misfire I remembered something that I tend to forget on a regular basis: I suck at flings. The rayon shirts they require start leaving rashes. I quickly dressed and dried, stuffing my underwear into my jeans pocket, and prepared to lean into her kitchen and make a hasty good-bye.

"Have coffee," Angie commanded, handing me a mug of piping hot Folgers.

We sat on her sofa. She reclined, mug and saucer in hand, and crossed her feet on my knee. I slowly eyed the length of her tanned runner's legs up to the hint of sheerly sculpted pubic hair that disappeared under her robe. The periscope under my belt violently reared up. Now you're ready, you little son of a bitch, I thought.

"I really should go," I said. "Have to work today."

"You told me you get horny when you work on weekends," Angie said.

I laughed nervously, squeezing my pockets to make sure I stowed everything I came with the night before, including my balled-up shorts.

"Can I call you tomorrow?" I asked.

9.

I was in an ethics trap. I couldn't dump Angie outright. Not now. That would mean tagging myself as a shallow, out-for-sex pig that disappears after he gets his fill. And, naturally, I am not that. That kind of behavior disgusts me. I could testify to a Senate committee about how much that behavior disgusts me. "It disgusts me, Mr. Chairman," I'd say, my hand atop a Bible and the microphone feedback piercing the stuffy chamber.

But how to get rid of her? I kissed her mouth, ran down the hallway into the elevator, and sifted through my options.

The most watertight strategy was also the most cowardly, yet it had a track record. I'd get her to dump me. I'd weasel out of the relationship. Namely, I'd taper off my interaction with her until we reached mutually blameless noncontact. Or until she unloaded me. Weaseling out rarely fails because it only requires a smidgen of self-esteem from one party. Women do it, too. I've had it done to me at least twice. That made it fairish. And since Tom had nixed using the semi-but-could-be-exaggerated-to-full-time-lesbian angle in the column ("*GQ* just did it," he informed me), her column potential was seriously stifled. The "performance anxiety" I had enjoyed with her might have been a column-worthy incident, especially since it could be sincerely misreported as a terrifyingly isolated case that had never happened before and would never happen again. But reporting that to 1.7 million readers, and every future date, seemed like a brilliant thing I could do after I ran out of many alternative ideas that might be more brilliant.

"Cookies for you," the office receptionist said on Monday morning, handing me a white bag she took the liberty of opening. *Good luck with your deadlines*, the card read. Chocolate oatmeal. Homemade. Angie was a semi-lesbian who baked. I guiltily ate five. I had not called Angie in three days, and now I had an hour of baking and a thirty-five-dollar messenger fee on my conscience.

She wasn't making this easy. So I enacted the second part of the strategy. I took the minimum action necessary to keep the ruse going by making a date with her—one that would be a noticeable downshift in time and intimacy from our previous outings.

Angie and I met at Chili John's (no entrée over eleven dollars) on Thursday night, and I sprang for cheese nachos. As usual, we stopped at her apartment, and were soon sitting atop her sofa in the *American Gothic* TV-viewing position. She killed the TV and clicked on the Natalie Imbruglia CD. If the choreography of the first several dates was any indication, we'd be naked in five minutes.

"Oh, I don't think I deserve you tonight," I said, drumming my knuckles on my knees. "I mean, after being so distant this week."

"You were busy," she smirked.

"No, I'm a moody son of a . . . gun, sometimes," I scowled. "I would not put up with that if I were you. No ma'am."

She wormed her toe into my zipper.

"That's why I like you, dating guy," she growled.

I explained that I had the monthly emergency phone meeting with the Sydney office at five the next morning and bolted. The first time you turn down sex is a pivotal point in weaseling out, I reminded myself speeding home. Now she'd have the tiny suspicion that I'm seeing someone else, or mentally ill, or a closeted gay, and I'd shortly be home free. Unless she called the next day.

"What the hell was wrong with you last night?" she screeched into the phone. "You've been acting like you're not interested anymore. And you know what? If that's the case, it's not like I don't have better opt—"

"What?" I said incredulously. "That's crazy. Everything's good with me. Wait a minute . . . hold on . . . Angie, are you not happy with something?"

She told me to call her apartment later. I dialed her work number at 9:45 P.M. and hit pound to skip her message.

"Angie? Are you home? Pick up if you're home. Angie? . . . All right, I'll talk to you on Monday. I won't be home this weekend."

On Monday I had an e-mail from her informing me of my mistake. Our communication was getting more abstract! Spinning to the far files on my chair, I caught sight of her cookie card, crinkled beside a crushed milk carton in the wastebasket. It was written in a beautifully, loving girly handwriting, made even more girly by the fact that she fooled around with girls. It was a note from a womanhood collective.

You spineless pantywaist, I burned, guilt eating holes in my intestines. Weaseling out kept my hands clean, and avoided having an insult spat in my face that I couldn't counter. It preserved my self-view as a principled man who, maybe like my father, could tell his teenage daughter what kind of man to distrust and not have a thumb pointing back at himself. It's yellow, but it's also feebly pretending to be the non-using guy I hoped to become. How many more times will I do this to a woman? I thought.

After a few more neutral conversations, and another short drinks date, it seemed to be done. Angie left a phone message saying, "You're more than moody. I hope you'll call me."

I didn't. But I could, which is another positive aspect of weaseling out. I could phone her a few months from now, curious about her well-being, purposely—or after some months, genuinely—foggy about who pulled away first. Weaseling out lets you leave without saying good-bye, so there's no eating crow if you try to come back. But that's not likely.

Polecats do have their pride.

CHAPTER TEN

A Merry Road to Ruin

1.

It made no sense.
None whatsoever.

Where is the money going? I thought. By any conservative accounting, the scratch paper and calculator declared, I should have been running a surplus of forty-one dollars per week, after all expenses. Instead there was a 284-dollar deficit.

This was the accountancy of doom. Sooner or later, invariably sooner if these figures held, I'd be a vagrant looking for a low-lipped trash Dumpster to relieve myself in, other than the one I was calling my new permanent address. I regretted every errant dollar I had wasted unnecessarily in the last thirty years. Just the other day I had given a bartender (a male one, yet) twenty dollars because he had hustled to keep a date and myself in drinks during a slamming dinner hour. That date was Daria, a woman who had sought me out on Match.com (this was still the source of about 90 percent of my companions). Dinner and alcohol ran seventy-eight dollars, before I doled out Jackson like I didn't need it. The crinkled receipt from an Irish pub was sitting before me on my dining table, since it was tax time. I remembered getting it last week and thinking it was light; dinner out with Daria—any woman—usually ran a good fifty bucks more than that.

Well, there's your answer, Feynman, I reflected. Dating was financially disemboweling me, to understate it. In this way I was in the solid fraternity of men, who well know the monetary bloodletting that trying to find—or keep—a woman requires. The exceptions are those lucky men who somehow, though guile, pluck, delinquency, and cunning, find women who will not only overlook the fact that these guys don't have a dime or never spend a cent on them, but will also pay their bills for them. I'll never forget sitting at a restaurant table overlooking the river canal in Lawrenceville, New Jersey, on a sublime July morning in 1999, having breakfast with a beautiful twenty-eight-year-old named Lori. She had great green eyes and punky blond hair, a delicious smile, legs that made every man stop speaking and break from thought for a second. "Billy got me into twenty-two thousand dollars' worth of credit card debt, because I was paying for everything to support him, and even letting him live with me," she revealed. "But I don't hate him for that, because if he had not done it to me, I would've done it to myself."

"Wouldn't you have rather done it to yourself?" I asked. "I mean, then you would have at least been buying stuff for yourself."

"It was worth the lesson," she would only reply.

I marveled at this. I wanted to find this dude Billy, tell him what a piece of garbage he was, and then ask him how in the hell he got this beautiful-ass girl to not only have sex with him whenever he desired, but to also financially eviscerate herself in taking care of his good-for-nothing self by paying every expense he had. How? I'd settle to have a girl like Lori and only have her pay her own expenses; that alone would probably save me over 270,000 dollars during a three-year relationship. I understood that Lori's codependence was likely of such a pathologically advanced degree that she was easy prey for a user like Billy, but good God . . . I could learn. Maybe this is what the *Men's Health* editor had alluded to when he recommended trying an experiment in which I treated a woman like utter dirt to see if she would thrive on it and ask for more. Maybe it wouldn't just compel her to put out, it would also make her shell out. What could be a higher pinnacle in female snagdom? A wife who was a husband whenever it suited you. An ATM and bill-handler who would only accept sex, and lots of it, for her services.

In not hearing Billy's side of the story, I might have been exaggerating the Holy Grailness that Lori presented to him, but I doubt I was far wrong.

"Why did you, in God's name, do that?" I asked Lori.

"I thought I loved him," she answered.

You sly-ass dog, I thought. This guy was good.

2.

Women tend to have little clue about how expensive dating is for a man.

"What, a few dinners?" they reply. "Okay, maybe flowers. Some show tickets and whatnot, okay. Drinks, whatever. Trips? Yeah, a hotel or rental car, but only once in while. Parking? Who gives a damn about parking? What is that, fifteen bucks? He drove. And by the way, all the dinners, he's eating, too. Nobody's twisting his arm to pay the tab."

"And it's not like I don't pay for anything," they say. "But I mean, come on, he's taking me out. And if he's going be cheap now, it'll only get worse if we actually got serious. Besides, I mean, am I not worth it?"

This is a composite response from about three hundred women who've spoken frankly to me (or so I believe) about the cashola topic, whom I met through dating, seminars, Web sites, and other various avenues.

This response is the healthy response.

The many women who have a damaging and categorically unhealthy view of courtship financing will say, "Uh-uh. No way. I pay my fair share. I'm not gonna let him pay for my dinner on the first date, or the first three dates or whatever. Why should he? I work. I can afford it. It should be equal."

The "Am I not worth it?" women find it utterly unbelievable that these women actually exist. "You are crazy," they will admonish them. "Well, at least I'm independent. At least I'm not using a guy as a meal ticket," the second faux-egalitarian chick will respond. "Independent? You're saying I'm not independent just because I'll let some guy pay for dinner? Listen honey, maybe you have to pay to get a guy, but I—"

It degrades into this. I've hosted this argument in about thirty online dating seminars. It lets me stop talking and sit on a desk for a good three minutes, and it's good entertainment.

3.

The cliché is fulfilled about 70 percent of the time. The better-looking woman is the "Am I not worth it?" woman in around three out of four cases, and the "I can afford it" woman is the hotter one in about one out of four cases. (I keep track of several dysfunctional things.) When the more attractive woman is taking the "I'm not a gold digger" stance, she will often clarify that she doesn't want a guy to spend his money on her if she isn't really attracted to him and she knows that things are not going to progress, so this keeps the affair as non-sticky and uncomplicated as possible. The opposing women will then attack the implication that they're screwing every guy who buys them a *panini* or else leading on these hapless rubes, and more arguing ensues.

The reason the "Am I not worth it?" women have the healthy viewpoint? Because, of course, they *are* worth it. If a guy doesn't think that, for reasons noble or not, he wouldn't keep spending money on the broad. He's dishing his money out because he's financing a campaign to win something he thinks is worth a big fight and significant sacrifice . . . and if he doesn't think so, why the hell would he value it if he won it? The fact that courtship is fundamentally one-sided, at least in regards as to who funds it, has been true since the first single-celled organism looked at another one and said, "I have a yacht." When gravity and biology are working properly, the man's mission is to pay and the woman's mission is to keep him interested enough to keep paying. If both partners have their choice of people, this can be a vigorous job for both of them. This leads to children and mortgages and a guy who says, "she was worth it," and a woman who says, "he was worth giving my youth and my fertility."

The "Am I not worth it?" woman, no matter how egotistically delusioned she may be about the enchanting experience a man enjoys while being in her company, has the healthier stance for three reasons. First, if this woman is going to find a man who will love her, she'd be wise to find a guy who believes—or shares the delusion, if that's the case—that she is indeed worth it. Secondly, the men who prostrate themselves by continuing to pursue her and pay for the honor of doing it, without demanding her to reciprocate with bedroom sessions or by accepting a ring at some reasonable point, serve important purposes: they show other men that she's being hunted, and they help her gauge her own mate-value, because she at least knows these hand-licking idiots are not worth her time. (While I have sympathy for aging singles who are duped by introduction services, guys who serve as willing meal tickets to pretty women—or women who tell them up front it'll be nothing but platonic—are often just johns to asexual prostitutes; they're getting something out of the deal, and if they want to keep paying for whatever that something is, it's on their head.) Thirdly, making the guy shell out dough gives

him a clear and traditional path to court her, and that is helpful to many uncreative, straightforward guys who need a clear
path and appreciate it.

When the "I can afford it" women argue their position to
the men in the room, asking, "Wouldn't you rather have a
woman who didn't expect you to pay?" the men make sounds
as if they have gas. "Yes, except no," is pretty much their response, because we as men do not know what the frig to make
of a woman who doesn't want us to pay. "You're basically saying you're not interested in the guy, because you don't want
him to feel as if you have any obligation to him for buying you
dinner," we answer, which befuddles and irritates these women
greatly. "That's not what we're saying at all!" they scream.
"We're saying we think we should both extend ourselves, that
it's a two-way street, we should meet you halfway [there are
dozens of these clichés, I've learned], not that we're not interested. We're saying it should be equal."

The men in the room look at each other knowingly, the
"Am I not worth it" chicks primp smugly, and the "I can afford it" women huff with anger, frustrated that they're not
being understood. Except it's they who don't understand.

Equal doesn't help us in the slightest, the men in the room
transmit to each other with resigned looks. It doesn't give us
one goddamned thing to work with, and they think they're
doing us a favor.

4.

The problem that's illustrated so vividly in these arguments in my humble little dating seminars is, in sum, that

dating among single Americans in their late twenties, thirties, and forties has one foot planted in our current time, and the other foot is firmly in 1926.* We're working with anachronistic customs that people can disregard or hold to as they wish, and this is chiefly why dating has become unbelievably fucked-up in the last fifty years.

We've done it to ourselves, mainly in the name of good.

First, obviously, the 1926 system that still governs the majority of our courtship thinking depends on a simple economic factor: The man didn't just have to cough up the cash to entertain a woman to impress her; he had to cough up the cash to prove he had it. In most cases, his paycheck would be their sole source of sustenance as a couple. She might make a few bucks a week sewing gloves together in a tenement factory, or typing reports for some fathead in an office, but mainly his earning power would dictate whether their lives sucked or not.

Picking up the tab is our way of saying, "I have money to blow on a partner, and I'll gladly blow my money on you because I want you to choose me over every other man." It meant that in 1926 and it means that now.** It's one of the

*Not specifically 1926, but any time that presented a reigning patriarchal situation in which men had the best prospects for earning money, women were financially dependent on men, and most Americans married in their early twenties. This set of factors still lingers in areas in the United States, especially south of the Mason-Dixon Line. I'm not talking about some sweet halcyon time in which Harold would don his best bow tie and go a-courtin' by knocking on Mary's front door with chocolates and posies in hand; people prone to recall such nostalgia tend to forget that Harold was a drunk with a second-grade education and Mary gave half the county gonorrhea.
**Using dinner solely as a trade for sex—"he buys'ya a little dinner and thinks he owns'ya"—is actually a rare use of a restaurant tab. Only extreme lowlifes

few customs that is still black and white for men, at least in
our view. And it's black and white in the majority of women's
views, as well. Most of the "I can afford it" women will, if
pressed long or hard enough, admit that they'd actually be ap-
palled if a guy relented to them on a first date and said, "Well,
okay . . . your half is seventy-two bucks." Men know this.
Women know we know this. That's why only schmucks (and
amazingly gifted, lucky guys like Billy) don't pick up the tabs
early on.

While most women still appreciate and/or demand that
men pay their way on dates, they, most obviously, no longer
need us to pay. They probably went further in college than we
did, got better grades, and are making the same money, if not
a bit more. (I'm not going to open the worm can about gender-
wage disparity; it exists, but women make quality-of-life
choices that slightly drive down their wages—he picks cardi-
ology and insane hours, she picks dermatology and an eight-
to-seven life; she waits tables off the books, he jackhammers
asphalt on the books, etc. It suffices to say that the average
middle-class, employed twenty-nine-year-old single woman
is a roundabout financial equal to her twenty-nine-year-old
male peer in the office cube across from her.)

And for that guy, this fact totally, completely, blows.

Not because female subjugation tickled us so, but because

(rich or poor) really think this. Usually it's a misunderstanding. It's easy for a
woman to assume a guy thinks she owes him sex for buying dinner, when really
the guy is the type who would've pushed for sex at any opportunity, which just
happened to come after dinner. She may also assume it wrongly when a decent-
intentioned guy just plain read her wrong, and thought she had let him take her
out to dinner (once, or fifty times) because she was digging on him and wanted
him to unleash the beast.

most of the dating rituals that we feel we have the slightest control over revolve around a women saying, "Okay, show me what you got," and us opening our wallet or our zipper.

What's in our wallet is much less likely to make a big impact on her now, unless it's very big indeed.

At least far bigger than hers.

5.

This economic freedom has granted new power in choice and options to women in relationships, and for men, it's made dating more challenging in several ways. Personally, I feel like somebody promised me I'd be able to feed myself if I learned how to spear fish, but then they took away my spear and I have to wade into a barracuda school with open hands.

Having chiseled abs would help the situation, I realize.

Undoubtedly, these changes in the dating power balance (caused by hundreds of factors influenced by our standard of living, global enlightenment, blah blah), have brought good things to women. Namely, a woman who's not a Miss America hopeful doesn't need to resort to marrying Earl from the neighborhood just because he's got a steady job down at the mill; she can survive with no Earl in her life quite well.

This woman—let's call her Celine—doesn't need to enter into an ill-conceived and/or abusive marriage with Earl, pump out a few kids, and then spend forty years trying to not think about how she might've done better if she had only been nicer to Eddie Salliwickie in the ninth grade, whenever being a parent and grandmother didn't distract her from her regrets.

On the flip side, Celine won't be forty-five, single and

childless, with a nice 401(k), and nothing but loads of scrapbook photos and jewelry baubles left in the wake of her dozen romances with Earls and Eddies, Toms and Chesters and Larrys.

The 1926 standards of courtship—which again, still apply greatly right now—highly favor young chickies. They are most powerfully apt when a twenty-three-year-old guy is pursuing a twenty-year-old woman, and spending a wad on her means dropping half of his 190-dollar part-time paycheck to take her to the Olive Garden and to a movie (if you think this dinky little date could not possibly cost that much, you are a woman).

Why?

You have a perfect storm of naïveté, parity, and demographic supply and demand at their ages. And it's fleeting.

But I must explain. These are my own observations, I will hazard to preface once again, and they come from talking with hundreds of singles in their twenties to, well, near death, as well as reading a crapload of social science research in the last decade, chewing the fat with a mass of relationship-type PhDs, trying to be observant about what is occurring around me, and synthesizing this with the glue of thought and an IQ that, when it was last tested in second grade, nearly broke three figures.

Warning: You may want to go buy a quart of Gatorade and grab a sandwich. This journey of elucidation (please forgive me, I've been reading one of P.G. Wodehouse's *Jeeves* novels and should not have done that while engaged in composition) and hypothetical example will involve, as the Irish say, a good stretch of the leg.

First, this twenty-year-old woman is near the peak of her beauty, highly fertile with several childbearing years ahead of her, and she has relatively few women around her who are serious mate competitors; they're mainly her same-age peers, or those women a couple years younger or older. Let's say there are fifteen thousand single men in her geographic area and circle of contacts (think of the Kevin Bacon game) that she'd consider dating (men aged nineteen to twenty-nine), and maybe another three thousand (men aged up to forty-five) who could have a chance at her if circumstances were right. Her boyfriend is physically in the most attractive 25 percent, though he's in the bottom 25 percent as far as wealth and about average as far as future earning power. Financially, she has nothing except her family's money.

This twenty-three-year-old guy she's dating? He's just coming out of the years when he was a walking gonad, ready to hump everything without sharp edges, and can ejaculate seven times in an hour. (Confirmed and archived.) He's got a pool of about say, eight thousand single women he could readily date (aged eighteen to twenty-six), and his girlfriend is in the most attractive 10 percent. Financially, he doesn't have a pot to piss in, but he'll start working soon. He's still impulsive and spontaneous, without roots, and is enjoying the vestiges of an immortality complex. He contemplates the forever nature of marriage and having kids about the same way that he contemplates taking a bullet for his country; he's ready, if it comes to that, and he doesn't really believe the worst outcome is the likeliest one to happen to him.

In 1957, these crazy kids would've almost assuredly made hip sparks and dashed into the wild thicket of marriage, him in a white jacket and Buddy Holly specs, her in gloves and lace, both squinting at the 8-mm floodlights and waving. They both had nothing but each other, a couple of high school diplomas and maybe his fresh bachelor's degree. And, hell, all their friends were doing it.

Now, let's fast-forward fifty years.

The same (well, except for tattoos, a couple of piercings, and clothing that intentionally reveals side tit and anal cleft) twenty-three-year-old guy and twenty-year-old woman are dating now, much like they did in 1957, doing the same things in a Toyota Tercel that their vintage doppelgängers did in a DeSoto. They enjoyed the same vast swell of potential partners as the 1957 couple did by attending a university, where they were drowning in dating opportunities every single frigging beautiful day. And they chose each other. Just two American kids, doing the best that they can.

Except they don't marry.[*]

He takes an office monkey job in finance and starts MBA classes, and then gets transferred to Minnesota, finds another job, and starts to make some cash, but getting ahead requires licensing classes and international travel. He dates around.

---

[*]The average age that Americans get married has been rising for many decades; it's nearing the late twenties for both genders, an increase of about five years from 1960. It's even higher among college-educated Americans, as any turn of your head will reveal. When you push up education, income, and other standards of living in that special first-world way, the marrying age retreats further into adulthood. To put it simplistically, this is because marriage is largely an act of the heart, not the head, or at least it should be (the opposite situation isn't the stuff of Hollywood musicals, I've heard anecdotally). By 2060, I predict that the average age that American men and women first marry will be fifty-one and forty-seven, respectively. If you have a bunch of actuarial tables and other data that contradicts this, I also predict that you'll be dead by then.

She gets her BA, then moves to Oregon to get her master's, gets an entry-level job in marketing, and then works on getting promoted to division assistant manager, which requires travel. She dates around.

Now he's thirty-three and she's twenty-nine. They both own starter homes in separate areas of the country. They both make between fifty-five thousand dollars and seventy-five thousand dollars a year, and both have at least thirty-five thousand dollars in a retirement plan. He's three years away from being vested in a pension. She's seriously eyeing a management job with a competitor, which will boost her salary by eighteen thousand dollars but require sixty-hour weeks at minimum.

They've both dated and slept with between eight and twelve partners, including each other, dating each for spans between two weeks and four years (including the three years they dated each other).

He's forty-five pounds heavier than he was a decade before, and he's lost half his hair, but he's still considered okay-looking. She's thirty pounds heavier than she was a decade before, but she still gets hit on quite a bit.

(Stick with me, I'm getting toward the end of it.)

Marriage, declarations of gayness, asexuality, and freak deaths have winnowed the single pool for both of them in the last ten years, and of course the paradise of college plenty is now only a memory viewable on soft-porn DVDs.

She isn't moving. Families make up a large percentage of the population in her suburban area, but she still has about ten thousand single men in her circle of potential contacts who she would consider dating. These men are aged twenty-six to fifty and make between fifty thousand dollars and two hundred and fifty thousand dollars a year. However, each of the men who she sees as a potential partner has between five thousand and twenty thousand single women who they could date, and she is only in the most attractive 40 percent.

She wants to get married, and is competing for a mate with every single women who is about seven years younger and four years older than her.

Let's look at her old college ex. He has about ten thousand single women around him he'd date, aged twenty-two to thirty-five (he does not care about their yearly salary). Financially, he's in the top 40 percent of his peer group, where he also ranks looks-wise. He wants to get married, and is competing for a mate with men in the span of ten years younger and twenty years older than him.

They both regard marriage as a huge, big deal, because they've seen friends devastated by divorces and custody battles, and they both have some money and a house to think about. Plus, they haven't stayed single this long without enjoying the perks of ruling their own roost. And that's addictive.

6.

This epic journey is a long, stultifying way of demonstrating that women give up a tremendous amount of dating leverage when they don't marry in their early twenties. Having financial freedom and the power of greater choices is a boon, but by the late twenties, women start to enjoy these dating choices in an increasingly shrinking pool of men, and they're also competing with an ever-growing number of younger women for these men.

On the other side of the chromosomal gap, when a man doesn't make an impetuous jump into marriage in his early twenties, his options obviously grow. One of his main sources of attractiveness—his wealth—will increase in the next ten years, while a woman's main evolutionary ammo—beauty and fertility, will . . . well, you know, remain steady. Yes, his wealth doesn't have the influence it once did, since women his age don't need his financial assistance to survive, but his moola is still the biggest cat's-eye marble he (and all men) have in attracting a woman.* He can also pluck further downward in the dating pool than women his age can, where the number of single women who lack any resources grow (and he can fish among the oldest students and postgrads in the university swell). Women can search for a mate among much older single men, but she'll have to compete with a large number of women for the choicest men.

When the dating seminars get around to this point, people are either sleeping, or in the bathroom, or they've either decided that they'd better catch an early train. The few women who remain look at me with a mixture of fatigue, interest, and disgust, as if they now understood something that had always been clear and self-evident to them just about as well as they

---

*I'd like to think this will change one day, when all women, black, red and white, Jew and gentile, will judge a man not by the size of his bank account by the content of his character. Or at least judge him less on the first and more on the second than they do now. But I acknowledge that these factors are often related and, well, poverty sucks. Actually, it might be better to forget all this and hope women's evolutionary skew toward materialism, even when annoying and snobbish, stays skewed. I could always strike it rich through dumb luck, whereas getting a new face or gaining a few inches of height through those painful shinbone-stretching procedures they give to four-foot Japanese women might take considerably more time and effort, as well as a lot of money to begin with.

ever had, but now they could borrow some different hypothetical examples if they were ever forced to explain it to
someone else.

Some of the women's looks—and voices—raise a note of
displeasure: "Great, you've just made me feel like dog shit in
knowing that I have to compete with—omigosh!—younger
women with higher tits and smaller asses for guys who are the
same simians I had drooling all over me fourteen years ago. I
also appreciate being reminded that even though I'm only
thirty-six—thirty-six, and I work out and still get hit on,
thanks very much—I'm only really hot to young guys with
some MILF* fantasy and men eighteen years older than me
who probably need pills to get it up. I remember some book
a few years ago about professional childless women who
'forgot' to have kids, which I purposely did not read, because I had a feeling it would have told me—surprise—that I
focused too much on my career and now I'm one of a billion
women who hear that ticking clock and doesn't have a guy
and is contemplating freezing her eggs or visiting a sperm
bank. Thanks for that illumination, really. Aside from
knowing this, what useful information is there in this? What
can I do about it?"

STOP USING THE SAME TACTICS YOU USED IN COLLEGE TO GET A MAN.

I tell them this, and most blink expectantly as if further
discussion is needed.

---

*Acronym for "Mother I'd Like to Know Better."

The single women who come to my online dating semi-nars—who are a little less proactive and often a tad bit more attractive than the female homo singolus found in singles mixers—typically rely on the same overall game plan of flirt-ing and attention-signaling that they have since their late teens/early twenties. It hangs on being available but reticent, and maneuvering in subtle ways to encourage a man to ap-proach. This is a perfectly smart and effective, and brilliantly evolved, strategy for a woman to use when her DNA thought she would be mating pretty much for good at age fourteen through twenty or so, depending on the variables of saber-toothed tigers and cholera. In the teens and early twenties, this woman has her pick of men who are young, dumb, and full of energy. There are single men falling out of every tree and every wall crack vying for her attention, so waiting for them to approach or subtly inviting a chase by doing very lit-tle is, really, all she needs to trouble herself with. And the guys she's interested in at this age are usually in the group of highly confident men who approach her most aggressively. The less attractive she is, the more aggressive she may have to be to get attention, but the odds still favor her. Especially now, when a teen girl has to be extraordinarily obese to be fat-ter than her high school peers.

A decade and a half later, she's still plying reticence and waiting for a "nice guy"—a more sedate, reliable, bill-paying, paternal-type dude—to approach her. And it's not happen-ing. Get a bunch of these "nice guys" in their thirties, forties, and beyond in the same room, and you'll readily learn that most are still scared shitless of approaching a woman, and the fifteen years or so since their atomic-wedgie humiliations haven't given him any more courage, though it has given them a smidge of indignant arrogance.

"Fuck her," some of these guys will say in the males-only seminars, their arms crossed defiantly, with others nodding. "If some thirty-nine-year-old broad is going to ignore me if I sit next to her in a Starbucks, or make it hard for me to start a conversation, she can go to hell. Who does she think she is? If she doesn't give me clear signals that she's not going to be some ego-stomping bitch, I don't need it. If she wants me to approach her, why the hell can't she just say something to me first? We're not sixteen anymore."

"If a guy thinks that I'm going to make the first move just to protect his frail little ego, he can definitely keep dreaming," women will say in the coed seminars, where the men, of course, nod in agreement to show that they haven't the slightest fear of accosting any female at any time. "If a man doesn't have the balls to approach me, then he's just done me a favor by not wasting my time or his. He's too much of a wimp to date."

All the women sound a huzzah, even those few in their early seventies. This argument is indefatible. Or at least it was.

"Ma'am, you're thirty-seven," I badly want to point out, but I'm sure it would get nasty letters sent to the administrators at the 92nd Street Y. "Your chief complaint is that you can't meet a guy you like, and every man who approaches you is not your type. The man you're looking for does not have the balls to approach you, nor the same inclination he might have had when you were a size six. I've met him. Many hims. You can't swing a belt without hitting fifty hims outside. For

God's sake, change your thinking, drain your moat, and consider approaching this guy first. He'll take it from there."

Neither side wavers. The stalemate continues. I back away
slowly, hands up, testicles ascended, nice guy that I am.

7.

My 284-dollar weekly deficit was a problem. It meant that
if my spending kept up that pace, or my income didn't take an
upswing, I'd soon be attempting to sell crude charcoal
sketches of passersby in Central Park to finance my next Big
Mac. I didn't mention my niggling worry to Daria, the thirty-
two-year-old girl I was dating whom I met on Yahoo! Per-
sonals. I wasn't sure she'd be as compassionate as I may have
needed at the time.

"Stephen, my last boyfriend, had to be the cheapest bastard I ever met," she said to me, linking my pinkie finger in
hers as we walked. "He actually delivered my Valentine's Day
flowers to me himself to save money."

"Maybe he was pinched," I said, wanting to chew my
tongue off.

At dinner out, I looked around at the other couples at the
restaurant, seeing the women laughing and talking, the men
laughing and quaffing. My brothers. They understood. Each
of them was going to spend at least one hundred dollars
tonight, and it didn't look like there was a stockbroker among
us. Nobody was complaining. Just that silent look of split-
second sobriety upon opening the black vinyl check holder.
Sometimes it was only a snap of arithmetic to count entrées or

tabulate the tip, but other times, Christ, I recognized it so clearly. It was the internal deep breath that said, "No . . . problem, it will be all right. You will make it. You always do. Pay it and hope you'll forget about it. You've always made it."

I was not making it.

Three weeks later I was walking near Lincoln Center; it was a raw autumn day. My bank account was overdrawn by 3,470 dollars. More than a month's mortgage. Way more. This does not happen to an adult man, I said to myself. I reminded myself that I was not indigent quite yet; I could raid my 401(k), and then eke out another five or six months of life before that ran out and then I'd simply kill myself. Like a samurai cutting his stomach, except I'd buy a .45 or jump in front of the F train.

See, that's the difference between a real man and you, I burned. You'd kill yourself like a sniveling little coward, while a man like that dude Billy would go make some chick like Lori pay all of his bills and like it.

The clouds in the fall sky were a roil of violet, red, and saffron—the kind of sharp, stringy clouds that looked like they stretched from the tip of your hand to seventy thousand miles away, and were so delineated by the low, 6:40 P.M. sun that you'd swear you could run on their edges if you were up there.

They were wilderness, oblivious to my overdrawn bank account, just like the crush of faces, traffic, signs, and people selling shit around me. I have no money, I thought. For a good five years of my adolescence, my family had zippo cash, and much of it was a bad time. There was not much of the "Well, at least we got each other" type of crap you see in movies or hear from people who never had money, or have been up and then really hit bottom and realize that it won't kill you. It was only a cold, purgatorial dread in which there was worry, some relief, worry, next week's check, and hope and fear that nothing happens to make things fall completely apart in a very public way. I'd bet this is very apt to strike modest middle-class families who have always paid their bills, think they ought to have enough to pay their bills, and have no idea what kind of horrors will besiege them when they can't.

I had no interest in revisiting that existence. I'd spent twenty years trying to gain distance from it. Now the swings between denial and hyper-alarm were becoming manic, with absurd swings between lavish wastefulness to prove I was an expanding universe away from those lean years in the early 1980s, and frugal measures to avoid sliding back to that abyss. I'd have a seventy-dollar steak dinner, then spend twenty-five minutes pulling the stove away from the wall to grab a quarter spackled with furry grease. I had the thought of Charlie Chaplin in *City Lights*, wearing a gifted tux and driving that roadster the drunk millionaire had given him, slowly following a man with a cigar waiting for him to toss it, and then jumping out of his car and pushing over an astonished bum to retrieve it off the sidewalk. You can put a tramp in a tux and a new car, but he's still a tramp. The tiny moral that the little tramp always knew the sun would still rise the next day, come whatever, made me relate to him about as much as I related to Lori's old beau Billy.

Contemplating ruin—or at least my megalomaniacal, ego-centric version of ruin, which did not involve actual hunger nor a deprived child but rather some humiliating backslide to dependence and a public admission of failure to justify my seat at the big-boy table of competitive adulthood—gave me just the slightest taste of what a city can become when you're, let's say, falling behind.

Looking around me at Lincoln Center, the hurried, oblivious faces all seemed to take on the look of annoyed landlords. New York would be a cold, foreboding place that offers no shelter, no respite, no compassion to those running short on financial oxygen. It was like floating in the middle of the Atlantic Ocean on a gray, silent day, the water not too choppy, a school of well-fed and wholly disinterested blue sharks all around you that, if they got bored or had nothing else to do, could always eat. But not now. Not while you still have some air in the life jacket and warm blood. Some kick to you. Maybe you'll panic. Or just float, trying to keep your head just above the cold water. No matter. You'll tire. They can wait. There's only one way this will go, and it will be much easier then.

Maybe I should think about taking on a couple more freelance assignments, I reasoned.

8.

Daria and I were relaxing on my couch, watching my TV, both of which would not be repossessed if I kept hitting the keyboard instead of drinking at Matt's Grill on random weekday nights. She was talking about a job interview she had in the coming week.

"They will find that I will fit in very nicely there," Daria said. "I will be covered in Prada from head to toe."

I knew exactly what she meant. I knew she didn't mean it

to sound like the starving masses of the world should shoot her or toss her in the basement if there's some sort of *Doctor Zhivago*–like coup. Daria's a woman, with four hundred pairs of identical black boot-shoes and a credit-card balance that would be a sweet Lotto windfall. She worked hard, and she couldn't walk around in the same jeans and Gap shirt that I did every day and expect to kick ass in the circles she knew. She reminded me a bit of Grace Kelly in the first half of *Rear Window*, while I reminded myself nothing whatsoever of Jimmy Stewart. Her world was a materialistic, exterior-based world, where something called Prada really mattered and was a big deal. But there's something diabolical in this, something that isn't akin whatsoever to the nice girl who wants to feel pretty at the prom with her pretty prom dress her dad had to work five weeks to afford, which is the condescending view I take of acceptable materialism. Perhaps it was her intonation that Prada wouldn't just be an advantage, but a minimum standard. There weren't just average Janes and winners in the circle she wanted to enter, there were losers who'd be expelled for being non-Prada types. And those girls could go die. It turned the image of the pretty prom girl with the blue-collar father into *Carrie*.

"You'll look great," I said, hoping we'd order a pizza instead of going to a restaurant.

CHAPTER ELEVEN

Humble Pleas From a Single American Man

1.

As George W. Bush told John Kerry in the 2004 presidential election, "a litany of complaints is not a plan."

Such an outlook fails to take into consideration just how good listing a litany of complaints can make you feel. "A litany of complaints" is an incredibly apt and complete definition of life, one that's far more accurate (and upbeat) than the veil-of-tears crap.

I have been on more than two hundred and fifty dates in the last six years.

I have a litany of complaints.

Of course, the perks far outweigh the hassles, which is true of most things worthy of carping and nitpicking. But, on behalf of my fellow single American male peers (it would be more proper and responsible to only speak for myself, but that cuts the self-righteous enjoyment of litanizing), I feel the need to criticize. I must judge.

So instead of just listing the litany of complaints, I've turned them inside out and phrased them as requests or demands for single women to start doing or stop doing the particular things that I, and all single men (and most married men, who also empower me to speak for them) everywhere on earth, find complaint-worthy.

There are thousands of smart guidelines and good, solid "Do's and Don'ts" pertaining to dating. Those don't interest me. The average rhesus monkey has the common sense to employ 99 percent of them. (Please don't ask me how I know that.)

The following requests/demands/pleas represent just a few eclectic things that single women do while dating that irritate me (us). Many are small things that drive men away, or slightly nuts, or toward the embracing balm of alcoholism or a long-awaited grave.

If single women will just take a few of these helpful suggestions into consideration, even just the last one, we could change the world. Or at least make a man here or there enjoy a date a smidge more and that could have incalculable ramifications, as demonstrated in *Back to the Future* and in the chaos-theory concept that a butterfly flapping its wings in Brazil can cause a tsunami in Tokyo.

I fully acknowledge that a large sect of single men (who I will call *them*, not *us*, because many are dopes) commit all of these transgressions—at least those anatomically possible or transferable to their gender—as frequently as women do. And even some of us, the decent and compassionate single men, do rotten and thoughtless things in dating that are nothing we'd like our daughters to know.

Finally, many single men will disagree violently with a few of these recommendations, at least outwardly, because they'd give us what we need instead of what we think we need desperately, at least in specific moments. I expect to be in that camp again soon, and rescinding several of the following pleas with impassioned arguments I'm working on improving right now. And I ask single women for some forbearance and tolerance and compassion.

Meanwhile, they need to do the following things immediately.

During the first date . . .

Wear earrings. What, it's too much trouble?

Ask a trusted guy friend for an honest, offend-me-if-you-have-to opinion about that perfume, body wash, or lip balm. A slightly disagreeable odor that's just a few atoms too heavy in deer piss or mashed posies can make a three-hour date feel like three days.

Don't answer your cell phone. On a first date men assume it's a planned call to give you an escape opportunity. Or another guy.

Don't start monologues that will eventually make me want to blow my head off. I'll let you talk about anything you want. Having you talk and talk and talk and talk is far preferable to the rigor mortis act. So I won't stop you, unless you've been talking about yourself or some uninteresting situation for so long that I need to step on your words to avoid sheer insanity. But please know that I am dying a slow death and would give anything if you would just . . .

Ask me one question. Just one damned question about me or my life. Don't spend three hours responding to my questions, talking enthusiastically about your own life, or waiting to be entertained. Asking a question that indicates you have some interest in my life, and letting me answer it, will put you in the top 3 percent of great dates.

Express open-minded interest in something I bring up that you have no interest in at all. I'm doing this for you constantly, so reciprocate just a little, i.e. instead of saying, "I don't watch television, so I've never seen *Leave It to Hitler* on cable and don't know anything about it [so change the topic back to me]," try, "I've heard about that show but haven't seen it—what's interesting about it?" See how easy?

If I talk on and on about myself, don't immediately assume I'm an egocentric conversation hogger who never shuts up; it might be because you're a vegetable, or you're letting uncomfortable silence persist after responding economically to my questions. Say something interesting. If I don't let you finish your sentences, label me an ass and move on.

Don't tell me about the conspiracies and evil schemes of your coworkers, whether you're a patent attorney, aerospace engineer, CVS clerk, or waitress. I don't know these people and I won't care about any of this drama unless it involves guns or sex.

If you're overweight, do not try to bring attention to it in some mitigating way, such as, "I broke my foot last winter and gained so much weight, I can't stand it," or "I'm on a new version of Atkins and I already dropped twelve pounds." All a guy hears is, "I'm sure you find my extra weight unattractive, but I'm hoping you'll overlook it." Pretend you really believe that you're attractive, without qualifiers. Every guy drooled for at least one enigmatic woman in high school or college (or right now), who was a good twenty or thirty pounds overweight but had the personality and magnetism to make her weight a nonissue. These women are rare, and I doubt it can be faked (the women I knew—Donna and Tara—were always heavy, from childhood on, but they always had "it"). Note that I'm not talking about a woman who's sixty pounds overweight showing a thong waistband; that's a brash, in-your-face middle finger to society that's nearly as capitulating as wearing a muumuu. But, honest to God, if Donna and Tara ever decided to show a hint of a thong (it would be fine lingerie, I'm sure), they'd make it sexy. How? I don't know. Pinning it on a quiet confidence or a vivacious personality is too simplistic. They weren't unique in those ways. Conventional beauty was only a small player in both of their cases. A hundred other women with the same body shape and weight as Donna and Tara would not get second looks. They had bottled magic. Voodoo. Think of one of these women that you know, or ask a guy about the one or two he knows, and try to reverse-engineer the chick. Good luck.

Don't try to pay. Don't do the feign where you reach for your purse or take your wallet halfway out of your purse when the bill comes, saying, "Oh . . . wait a second, here . . . wait . . . Are you *sure?*" We know it's almost certainly an empty gesture, or a way of diminishing our benevolence of buying you dinner by showing that you tried to talk us out of it but we insisted. (If you actually are solely trying to emphasize gratitude, this is the wrong way to do it.) If you asked me out, you can make a push to go Dutch or to pick up drinks without risking this negative overtone.

Learn how to kiss well. Or at least be better than the guy you're with. There are plenty of grown, pretty, highly datable women who are inept kissers. It's not fatal, but it sucks when the first portent of sexual activity isn't arousing or satisfying, especially if you want to do it for three hours. I dated a saving-sex-for-marriage virgin in college for a few beautiful months, and she showed me how hot good kissing can be. Sometimes I wish I had never met her.

Go right ahead and get naked, go down on me and have sex with me. If you have no interest in dating me seriously, and don't see any chance of us having a relationship, use me like the dirty whore I am. Unless I'm averse to getting physical with you, likely due to reasons that were not revealed in your blurry online dating photo from 1999, or other reasons all too obvious, I probably won't put up a rabid fight. Especially if you're absolutely insistent. Make coffee, too, please.

If we only had dinner, let me call you. If the date was an event in which I bought you some ticket or admission that cost twenty dollars or more (a play, opera, concert, wine tasting, anything above a movie), call or e-mail me the next day with a brief second thank-you (the first thank-you should have come at the end of date, though it's omitted quite a bit). Do this whether you want to see the guy or not. It's the class thing again.

Learn the art of polite direct rejection. Tell me, "I don't think we have the right mix to do the dating thing; I'm sure you may have sensed it as well." Don't just leave two calls unanswered so I get the hint. Have class.

A tip from the trenches: If a guy in your circle of friends wants to date you, and you're not interested in him but also don't want to destroy the group dynamic, consider being indirect. If you two have gone out once and he made slight overtures, or gone out twice with no overtures but he wants a third date, tell him about a guy you're interested in (who he doesn't know) and ask for his advice. He'll read you. He'll be less attentive to you, but the group dynamic should survive intact. If he doesn't back off, spell it out. Of course, this depends on personalities and history, and a direct rejection might be best in certain chemistries, but more often not.

If you think there might be a remote chance of us having a long-term relationship . . .

Do not tell me your timeline for getting sexual. Unless I'm going for your pants with flagrant dedication that won't be discouraged (which is a signal to lose me if you're looking for a husband), I don't need to know this. Telling me on the first or second date, "I never sleep with guys until we've dated at least a month—just my little rule," won't make me think you have especially high standards. It'll make me think you need artificial timelines because you don't trust your instincts. It can also create expectations. If I become a real jerk-off and push you into telling me when I'm going to get me some, be direct and say, "I'd like to wait until we've dated longer." If longer means more than a month, say so and why.

Do not go beyond topless on the second date.

Do not give me oral sex until we've had three dates.

Do not give me oral sex but refuse to receive it without saying why (even if you think it's obvious why, verbalize it). It's weird. I'll think you have some sort of complex.

Do not sleep with me until we've had four dates. Two dates is too soon if a man is a genuine long-term relationship candidate, and three can feel expected since sex on a third date is a cliché. If you think I just might be "the one" (how men hate that term), you're better off waiting.

Until we have had three dates . . .

Do not insult my black leather couch. It's been around a lot longer than you. And I can clean it with Windex.

Don't assume you're sleeping over unless you had to travel for more than forty minutes for the date. If you break this rule, you're probably having sex with me too soon.

Don't leave anything in my apartment. Don't forget anything. It's an ominous sign that you're going to be clingy or controlling, even if was purely an accident.

Don't tell me about abusive boyfriends or horrifying home/childhood situations or the story about your father and the wire clothes hanger.

Wait until we are dating seriously before you . . .

Start pressing the replay button. If you've already told me the story twice, and there are no new, highly interesting or critical details to add, please don't bring it up again. I might let you tell me the story again, and ask questions, and seem interested and concerned, but if it's something stupid that's not life-threatening or doesn't involve a dying immediate relative, don't put me through it again. Examples are a house flood, a problem with a landlord or insurance, a chiropractic issue, a feud with a parent or sibling over nothing interesting, your unbelievably inconsiderate roommate, plans for home decorating and reasons for each decision, the wealth of your extended family and their villas in Europe, and the like. When we're serious, I might develop antibodies to cope with repetitive stories, or I'll feel comfortable enough with you to occasionally ask you to just give me the PowerPoint version. I'll remind myself when necessary that women value the process of communication while men tend to overfocus on getting to the point or finding a solution. But if you do this in early courtship, I can still bolt and save myself.

Even consider the notion of condomless sex. Do not allow sex without a condom until we're fairly serious and we've talked about it. I might take you up on it, but I'll suspect that you're a reckless, VD-ridden fool. Not marriage material. If you think college-educated, professional women are too smart and careful to forego a condom with a new (or newish) guy, or that he'd really have to cajole her into it, or even be the one to suggest it, you're wrong.

Pull the "I'm pissed off at you but I'm not going to tell you why" stunt. If we've had less than six dates, and I do something that incenses you, either dump me or speak up. Do *not* attempt to make me figure out why you're angry. Just under severing a guy's penis with a carving knife, this is the most annoying trait you can demonstrate in early courtship. I know you'll do it occasionally if we get serious, since you're female, but if you do it in our early dating phase that means you will do it constantly. Few women have the charms to outweigh this negative, and most of them travel by private jet on someone else's dime.

2.

I'll probably never yell "nice ass!" at you from a delivery truck. But if I did do something similar to you once—you know who you are—I feel the need to explain myself.

And to offer a few words of enlightenment on behalf of the guy who yells this at you *every day*—and again I'm speaking for him fully without his approval or consent.

In other words, here are a few words about catcallers, and why they're your friend. About two years ago I volunteered with a charity that picks up unused food from New York restaurants, delis, schools, etc. and delivers it to homeless shelters and other food-needy places. My company had a "give back to charity" day, so I spent it driving around in a delivery truck with two guys. The truck driver was a man in his early 30s and the guy who retrieved the food at each stop (while the driver stayed in the truck) was perhaps in his late 20s. From 8:00 A.M. to 6:00 P.M., we drove up and down and throughout Manhattan.

Picking up food was job number 2. Job number 1, I instantly learned, was pretending to try to pick up girls.

At every light, every stop sign, every slow street, these two guys eagerly searched for a good looking woman and either made animated conversation about her, or leaned out of the window and gave her a few words. Sometimes they spoke softly ("Hey? Hey there? Baby?") and sometimes they yelled ("Just one night! That's all I want!")

They insisted that I needed to learn how to yell propositions at women, too, since I didn't look like I knew how to do it and that was pitiful. After cajoling me for four hours, they refused to move the truck in a busy intersection until I said something to a woman walking on Madison. Car horns were blowing in fury, cabbies were screaming, all hell was breaking loose. It was an odd form of blackmail. Thinking about the greater good, I finally leaned over and said, "Lookin' fine momma!"

She turned and looked at me, seeing me between these two guys in the front seat of that truck. She furled her brow in confusion. I desperately tried to communicate with her telepathically. She smiled, why I'm not sure. We finally started moving through the intersection. The driver slapped my back and told me not to fret, I'd get better with practice. "It'll come, man," he said. "It comes in time." I have to say that I felt a little proud. Like an agoraphobic who had run outside naked for five seconds.

I learned a few things that day:

1. This sounds horribly racist, and I wouldn't mention it unless it was confirmed in dozens and dozens of interactions (it was a long day and these two had coffee): African American women know how to deal with cat callers, and white women don't.

Every black woman who was catcalled (the driver was white, the assistant was black, and I'm white, for the record) turned toward us and said something along the lines of, "Excuse me? Are you talking to me, sweetie? Now what would you like to do again? No, tell me, c'mon . . ." This shut down my two truck buddies fast. The driver usually just looked back perplexed and hit the gas. Several other black women just smiled back with an "In your dreams" grin, which was confident and non-encouraging and also left these two guys with no comeback.

White women, on the other hand, pretended they didn't
hear anything, or stoically walked forward with troubled or
disgusted looks. Others glared back and then turned away
with a peeved sigh. These responses only encouraged these
two dudes to get louder and more aggressive. They expected the passive or blatant blow-off. It put them squarely
in their home court. They knew what to do with that.

2. This observation is also not all that nice, but it held
true in dozens and dozens and dozens (we actually didn't
finish until 6:05 P.M.) of occasions. The more visually attractive a woman was, the less harshly she reacted to a catcall. The less visually attractive she was, the more hostile
or troubled her reaction. I'm still struggling to think of any
logical connection here.

3. These particular two guys were harmless, if I had to
make a wholly uneducated instinctual guess. They weren't
vulgar, as far as dropping F-bombs or talking about orifices when they bellowed at pneumatic pedestrians. It
seemed like they viewed beautiful women with a detached
foreign regard; sort of like Jackson Pollack paintings that
might talk back to you.

4. I got the sense that it made their day far more bear-
able. (Yeah, duh.) Hurling propositions at women was like
a steam valve. Their jobs kind of suck, as far as autonomy
or diversion goes. There's a lot of monotony. The people at
the restaurant kitchens, delis, and schools usually treated
them dismissively or pretty ignorantly. Bill collectors called

the driver on his phone. People say catcalling is all about power. Sure. But for these two guys I didn't feel that it was specifically a "me vs. her" type of power flare, but more of 'me vs. life and look there's a hot chick' type of power flare. In catcalling, they can feel like an aggressor for a quarter-minute, or at least say what they're really thinking, without losing their paycheck. Catcalling among guys who have all the autonomy in the world and speak their mind anytime they want—maybe it happens just as often. Yes? No? I don't know. Maybe you know.

5. There was always a slight cognitive disconnect in see-ing a woman in a short, tight, slitted skirt, bare belly, and a sheer, skin-clinging top react somewhat harshly or become annoyed when these two guys said something to her. (Usually something fairly innocuous, like "Babeee!") A cognitive disconnect sort of like seeing a man walking with a sign that reads "LOOK AT ME" who screams "What are you looking at?!" when people stare. I know this sounds somewhat related to the famous sexist defense of rapists—she looked like she wanted it, and so forth. In the utopia of a completely non-objectifying society, these women would be looked at with either silent disregard or silent respect for their fitness by all strata of people. But I doubt that this so-ciety would procreate in any manner we'd recognize.

You could talk about the motivation, justification, or evilness of this cognitive disconnect for months, host inter-national symposiums on it with moderated panels, and on and on. But it's there. At times that day I felt my two truck seatmates and whatever woman was showing way too much skin were playing expected and interdependent roles, sort of like the coyote and the bulldog in those old cartoons who'd both punch in on a timeclock before doing battle. She exhibits, they catcall, and then they both punch out and go home until tomorrow. If only one of either showed up, the other might spend the day thinking "What, they call in sick?"

6. Here's a strategic tidbit, for whatever it's worth. Just as with the Oscars, you have a better chance of winning the "Ass of the Day" award if you're spotted later in the day, since the morning contenders (while recorded on fast food wrappers or clipboard form margins) start to fade from memory due to the sheer number of candidates.

They forced me to pick the winner at 5:56 P.M. with the same "we're not moving from this intersection" trick they used earlier to get me to catcall that woman on Madison. "Can't they all win?" I asked. They could not, I was told. This was just not done. So quickly (horns were blowing, cabbies were screaming) we narrowed it down to two: the woman walking outside of Staples and the woman at 5th and 65th. I chose the Staples woman solely so we'd start driving again, though she probably would've won anyway. I meant no slight to Ms. 5th or 65th.

7. In a few instances, there seemed to be—at least to this observer in the middle truck seat—a mutually perfect exchange between one of these guys and a pretty woman. She wasn't necessary gorgeous, but she had some intangible quality that made aggressive catcalling unthinkable. She'd be walking with confidence, emanating something formidable and welcoming at the same time, some quality that seemed to say, "I'm beautiful, you have eyes, and making me think you're a civilized man is worth everything on earth at this moment." The two guys in the truck usually watched her silently as she walked closer. (Okay, we all watched.) One of them might say, "Look at this chick!" when first seeing her in the distance, but then they'd mysteriously shut up and just watch. When she was near, the driver or assistant, whoever was closer, would say something like, "Hello." Just a second later than usual.

"Hi," she'd answer, smiling, not offended or grateful but she'd say it conclusively, with an atom's worth of returned flirtation. And with finality. Then she'd walk by and away. Nothing more would be said about her. These three women weren't even mentioned among the A.O.D contenders, and those nomination requirements were pretty liberal.

I have no idea of what kind of alchemy was at work with these three particular women, but they all had the same presence. And they all got the same reaction.

8. At the end of the day, after riding in that truck, I felt both relieved and a tad bit contemplative for most of the annoyed women we had bellowed at in the last 10 hours, in thinking that the guaranteed, universal cure for catcalling is the same one that an old barber used to tell me was the cure for a too-shirt haircut.

Just wait.

CHAPTER TWELVE

I Fear I've Been too Hard on Allentown

In looking over some of my comments regarding Allentown, Pennsylvania, where I lived from 1996 to 2001, I fear I may have seemed a bit harsh. It's actually a lovely place.

For starters, the women who cram around the shuffleboard table in P.J. O'Malley's pub don't give a goddamn about Prada, or at least don't talk about it if they do, which I didn't fully appreciate at the time.

Lehigh University and Lafayette College are there, so there's higher learning happening all around. And Easton, Pennsylvania, the birthplace of heavyweight champ Larry Holmes, is only about a twenty-five-minute drive on Route 78. Most of my relatives on my father's side are in Easton, as that's where my grandfather settled the family after emigrating from Sicily in 1924.[*]

---

[*]My father, aged nine, was strongly opposed to leaving his village in Sicily to live in America and made this known to his mother, father, brother, and two

Nearby Bethlehem (which some woman in a bar who sounded pretty sure of herself told me was really the town Billy Joel was referencing in his song "Allentown," since the steel industry was really based there, but "Bethlehem" didn't sound right as a lyric[*]) has a nice historic center. I even met Brian Setzer once at the Hotel Bethlehem bar. His tattoos made him stand out.

For full disclosure, I never actually lived in Allentown. I first lived in a small town adjacent to Allentown called Emmaus (ee-MAY-us), named for someplace in the Bible. It was where the publishing company was located. For the last six months of my Lehigh Valley experience I lived in another small Allentown border town called Macungie, which is an Indian (native-American type of Indians, not the ones from India) word for "the divide in the stream where the deer come to drink." I never saw the actual stream, nor any deer.

---

sisters during the entire weeklong ship voyage and the several days the family was detained in Ellis Island due to my grandmother's heart illness. In his photo, stapled to the third-class ticket for the ship named *Conte Verde*, his anxious expression seems to be saying, "This isn't funny anymore." My father did not enjoy his stay at Ellis Island, either. "They made you sit forever and then it was endlessly filling out forms." I tried to take him on a tour of Ellis Island in 1992. He declined, saying, "It would be like your son trying to take you to the DMV."

[*]This is also allegedly the reason why Paul Simon used Joe DiMaggio instead of his actual hero Mickey Mantle in the lyrics of "Mrs. Robinson," and why Paul McCartney used Jude instead of Julian in the lyrics for "Hey Jude" (the inspiration for the song was McCartney's desire to send some supportive, pick-me-up thoughts to John Lennon's son, Julian, who was having a rough time of it during Lennon's divorce from his mother). Allegedly.

CHAPTER THIRTEEN

The Borrowed Wife

1.

It's always there. Behind glass with a small placard that reads break IN CASE IT HAS REALLY COME TO THIS.

The word *prostitution* has such a filthy ring to it, unfortunately.

Walking up Eighth Avenue from Port Authority on Forty-first Street, at 2:00 A.M., it's not difficult to see why.

"Hey shorty—shorty!" a black woman in a short leather skirt and white boots will invariably yell to me, some times while trailing me closely for five steps. "You look like you're freaky, and I want to get real freaky tonight."

"I'm probably not all that freaky," I reply.

It never feels like the right time to give the woman a small lesson in marketing, but I always want to explain that if you want to impress a potential customer, you probably shouldn't start off by insulting his height.

2.

For plenty of men, crossing the precipice from enticing a woman into having sex to paying a woman for sex is, well, not a precipice at all. They traverse it about as easily as a crack on the sidewalk. I remember a magazine poll we did some years ago in which we asked men if they had paid for sex, and we expected perhaps 15 percent to say they had. It turned out to be slightly over 50 percent. Of course, we may have just caught all of the wrong guys on the right day, or some might have justified their answer with the old saw: "I'm married. I pay for sex every day."

I know a few men—respectable shirt-and-tie wearing family men with ostensibly happy marriages—who go to Nevada somewhat regularly and enjoy themselves with a lady of the desert.

"Don't you feel like you're cheating on your wife?" I asked one fifty-two-year-old guy once after being emboldened by five beers and a half hour of listening to his dude-ranch anecdotes.

"Absolutely not," he said, affronted. "If I was banging some girl at work, yeah, then I'd be cheating. But this is simple business, practical. It's clean, safe, without any strings, and I know this woman isn't going to call me some night at three A.M. screaming and threatening to blow me away or wreck my life."

"Oh," I replied.

This conversation took place before the "What happens in Vegas stays in Vegas" marketing campaign, but my coworker (same company, not same magazine staff, I had better point out) was arguing just that, with the addendum of "and she stays in Vegas, too."

Like any highly impressionable guy prone to long sexual dry spells, I reexamined my stance in light of his cavalier explanation, and still do every few months when I see soft-porn escort commercials on a local cable channel (flipping by it) or a smattering of ads in serious magazines showing a woman who looks just like the woman who lives next door to me, only she'll gladly knock on my door in about an hour if I'm waiting for her with about four hundred dollars (according to another shirt-and-tie friend who heard such prices quoted through the grapevine).

It's only practical, I'll mentally argue. Business. I might as well be buying envelopes from her. The kind of envelopes that will make me ejaculate for about four hundred dollars. And it's not like I wouldn't be in the company of many esteemed men. Hugh Grant. Eddie Murphy. Colin Farrell. Abraham Lincoln. JFK. And probably thirty-eight other presidents. Before the colloquial definition of America's essence was abbreviated to baseball and apple pie, "great whores" probably batted third. If we're the only country where capitalism truly works, there must have been some nod to the original work that inspired all capitalism.

I needn't even mention all the decent people in Amsterdam.

It's assisted porn, I rationalize. Is the slippery slope from buying a six-dollar magazine, then a nineteen-dollar DVD, then a four-hundred-dollar visit from a twentysomething girl who has student loans to pay and only wants to help really a slope that one should judge as slippery in the negative sense? Now that everyone has a 24-7 direct hot link to an inexhaustible free supply of the raunchiest pornography the human mind has conceived, via their friendly Internet provider, two things seem fairly clear. First, at least one out of every two women in America aged eighteen to eighty has made a video-taped sex scene with one to thirty men that is now on the Internet for everyone to see, including their mothers, fathers, priests, fiancés, and children or future children, so women obviously have no problem with it. Secondly, hiring a prosti-tute is efficient. You could waste hours searching for truly arousing free porn on the Internet, since only the most pitiful, pathetic losers on God's green earth would tap their credit card number into some pay-for-porn Web site run by a fat middle-aged dude named Dominic in the Cayman Islands. An actual lovely prostitute making a routine house call could do the job within twenty minutes, and you would at least know your tip was going in her pocket instead of some middleman's.

Why don't I have one after *plumber* in my Rolodex?

3.

Despite these sound reasons, crossing over the precipice to paying for it may be easy for many men, but it's still a daunt-ing gulch to me. I'd like to think that morality is mixed in somewhere with my aversion to it, and maybe also the fear of appearing on some HBO show about the Mustang Ranch in a segment after a bucktoothed teen thanks his momma for the birthday gift. But a lack of direct exposure is likelier a bigger factor.

The closest I ever came to hiring a prostitute—when I was

actually actively seeking one—was when I was seventeen. It was a team effort. A guy we called Schnepps was getting married (he was the twenty-three-year-old brother of the kid I hung with), and we all decided to throw him a bachelor party. During the bachelor party, which consisted of us drinking beer in his grandmother's Ben-Gay–smelling apartment in Gloucester City, we decided that we needed entertainment. All six of us crammed into Schnepps's sputtering, dented '82 Chevette, and took off for Camden.

Camden, New Jersey.

Stop by some time.

We found a likely prospect standing on the busy corner of Station Avenue, wearing red vinyl boots. She looked at us. She saw six faces in the gray rusted car. We looked back. This went on several minutes. Then she walked over. I felt my bladder tighten.

"You guys okay?" she asked.

We all peered at her. Twelve eyes, our heads crammed together. It was now or never. Her or nobody. Schnepps—the eloquent one—went for it.

"Will you take forty bucks to come and dance? Just dance. In an apartment right up the street. It's my bachelor party."

We looked at her expectantly. In the movie scene, she was supposed to jump in the backseat across our laps, give us all erections, and we'd drive back to Schnepps's grandmother's apartment laughing and whooping for the hottest seven-person bachelor party Gloucester had ever witnessed.

"I'm sorry?" she said, studying us.

Schnepps repeated it. A kid named Halsey added a "yeah"

at the end so he could say he did the talking. Her expression clearly showed that she was not apprehensive, which would have been understandable, or repulsed, which we couldn't have argued too much with, either. Or intrigued, which we kind of banked the whole night on.

She gazed at us with pity.

"No, I'm not interested. But thanks."

We were stupefied. I watched her eyes slowly track across the car and, as I feared, connect right with me. We were making eye contact. Her face seemed to say, "I expected as much from these idiots, but I am very disappointed in you."

"Will you do it for forty-five bucks?" Halsey said.

"Drive! Drive!" a guy named Daryl screamed. Schnepps floored it and we chugged onto Station Avenue and disappeared with angry puffs of blue smoke.

That was the entirety of my experience in soliciting a straight-off-the-street prostitute. So for years I felt like I had been there and done it, and knew pretty much all there was to know about the process. The following decades brought several run-ins with what I'll call quasi-prostitutes, who are strippers who dance in clubs or drop in on bachelor parties (sometimes with a 270-pound-guy who has a gun strap across his chest) and will provide oral favors or sex to guys who are willing to cough up extra dollars. (Again, to judge by the billions of clips available on the Internet, at least 30 percent of all American women have gotten freaky in this particular manner).

What, you're saving yourself? I would sometimes think, when a drop-dead beautiful, lovable, sweet, innocent, true-blue slip of a country girl with milk-fed dimples grinds her bare ass into my groin and asks me if I'd like to have more fun in the VIP room for the hundred- , two-hundred- , or three-hundred-dollar-options.*

Be a man. Take this filly into the back room and give her what she wants, one of the primal jackasses in my psyche says. He's the one with whiskey on his breath, a toothpick in his teeth, and trail dust on his calloused hands.

I wouldn't have lasted too long riding in Mexico with Bill Holden and Ernie Borgnine in *The Wild Bunch*.

4.

If you're a single man who lacks the moral depravity and/or intestinal fortitude to hire a prostitute, and you're on a long sexual dry spell, you do the next worst thing. Actually, most single, hard-up men attempt to do this before, during, and after any time they're considering the prostitute option, since it can happen serendipitously and is more societally acceptable.

You find a woman whom you're going to regard as a prostitute but not actually pay. And if she turns out to be a diamond, immediate sex may be the beautiful beginning of a life-changing relationship.

You go out to get laid. Single women do this as well. You just have to hope you meet one of them, and that the one you meet isn't going to make Norman Bates look like a college dean.

Put another way, this involves risks.

---

*This scale refers to orifices.

Serendipity seemed to be knocking, as well as drinking heavily and wearing a revealing blouse, at Cilantro's bar on the Upper East Side around 10:00 P.M. on a Saturday.

"Know anything about cognac?" a brunette on the next stool asked, squinting. She was maybe thirty-six, nice-looking.

"Sure," I answered, my mouth full of chips and salsa. "You can't go wrong with that one," I said, pointing.

"That's port wine," the bartender said.

I chewed slowly, looking at him. "Right. Or there's . . . that particular Courvoisier, over here. Might do that after quesadillas."

"Great. Have some?"

I stopped mid-nacho.

"Sure, absolutely."

Her name was Kat, short for Katrina. She was a buyer for a clothing chain. Born in Tennessee. She had a southern accent and two lustrous green eyes. I set the chip basket back on its bottom.

"People say I'm too trusting," she said as the bartender placed two howitzer-shell burritos in front of me. "But I think that's still good in times like these."

"Most definitely," I agreed. She touched my wrist with her finger.

"That's a really nice suit jacket," she said.

"Thanks," I shot back. "I bought it in Delaware."

She gave me her diapers-to-Dexedrine life story, eventually washing down her cognac with a tall cosmopolitan. Finally, she mentioned that she had no beau, something her mother disliked.

"Moms," I said, smirking, hoping to get a smile.

"Kiss me," she commanded.

"Here?" I asked. She puckered and closed her eyes.

Peck.

"Again," she ordered. "Again." Pucker.

Smooch.

"I like you," she said, touching my ear as she headed to the little cowgirl's room.

"She a regular?" I asked the bartender.

"Never saw her before," he said. "Love that accent, though."

Returning, she hopped in my lap. "Let's go," she whispered.

"Okay. Can I finish my tortilla?" I replied. She rubbed my upper thigh.

"Oh mahhh, what's that?" she asked, grinning. "What's that? Huh?"

"That's my cell phone."

"Wow."

"It's an old one," I said. She sucked down her drink, leaned over and whispered an obscene proposition. I looked at her green eyes, scanned her cleavage, smelled her perfumed neck. According to Blue Shield, I've only got forty-five years left. Why not? Hell, when you're lucky enough to stumble on the river of life, you'd better fill your canteen.

"No reason I can think of," I answered, breathing quickly. "Bartender, can you get a cab?"

We sped to an address she gave me. In six minutes, we stood on a dark corner.

"We're here," I announced. She kissed me and we skittered down into a wide doorway.

"Okay, so where do you live?" I said minutes later. No reply. Then, drunk, she clicked off like a morning streetlight.

"Look," I said, gently shaking her chin. "It's quarter of two . . . let's go inside."

"Let's play over your house," she giggled, fondling me. I thought hard. The olive skin atop her breasts was screaming to me. She laughed again, her breath sweet with Cointreau. Then she blacked out, still smiling, craning her neck gaped-mouth. Her thigh felt like a hot radiator hose. I pinched my eye sockets, squinting, letting coulds and shoulds wrestle. The last time I was in this situation, I was nuzzling an Alpha-Sig sweater.

"Christ," I winced, grinding my incisors. I shook her awake. "Look, let's forget it and get you home." She smiled and fell asleep again. We did this tango for another twenty minutes.

"Kat!" I finally yelled. "Goddamn it, I'm not leaving you here on the friggin' sidewalk! Now tell me your address . . . or . . ."

"Or what?" she teased, smiling.

"Or what?" I grimaced. "Or . . . I'm gonna call the cops! Now what'll it be?!" I glared at her sternly with eyebrow arched. She thrust her lips into mine. After several more futile questions, I angrily fumbled my phone free and hit 911.

"What's your emergency?" said an unsexed female.

"I'm with an intoxicated woman in a door stoop," I said.

"Hold for nineteenth precinct."

"Dougherty," said a hoarse guy with a heavy Brooklyn accent.

"I'm with an intoxicated woman in a door stoop," I repeated between groans.

"Good for you."

I explained the situation more fully. "Can you send a cruiser?"

"We're not a taxi service."

"She's getting . . . abusive."

"Yeah, I can hear that she's killing you."

He was not helpful.

"Did you call the po-lice on me?" Kat said, becoming momentarily lucid. Losing patience, I rifled through her black purse. No ID, but it did yield a tiny cell phone.

I dialed "Roy." Ten rings, no answer. "Judy and Martin"—

"Hello?" a sleepy, timid southern voice squeaked.

"Do you know a woman named Kat?" I said with peeved clarity.

"This is her mother! In Tennessee!" the voice screamed.

"Oh, Christ," I blurted. "Her mom?" I turned to Kat. "You call your mom Judy?"

The voice on the phone was in a panic. The radio therapist emerged.

"Ma'am, relax, your daughter is all right. She's laying in a door stoop intoxicated. . . ."

"Let me talk to her!" the lady shrieked. I held the cell phone against Kat's ear while she made pre–vomiting faces. She didn't respond to the screams coming out of the cell phone.

"Judy, I know this is a call that no parent wants to get. But if you can tell me her address or who to call to—"

"How do you know Kat?!" she burst, hysterical.

I explained that we had met recently.

Judy whimpered in deliberation. For two long minutes. She was alone and had to decide.

"I cannot tell you what to do at this moment," the radio therapist said to her. "I can't say I would give a stranger this information. But she won't leave the sidewalk."

"Well . . . you don't sound like a man who'd . . ."

"Certainly not," I agreed. An hour ago, when she was coherent and mobile, maybe. Now, no. The broad was a total mess.

After a twenty-minute taxi ride, I carried Kat into her bedroom over-the-altar style. I laid her on her bed. She opened her eyes.

"Why'd y'have to call my mom?" she slurred, pounding her mattress. "Why didn't you just take advantage of me? God. Hey, wait a minute," she said, trying to unbutton her black sweater. I was having Mimi flashbacks. No flip-flops were in sight, though. I knelt down and kissed this woman's forehead. She scratched my stomach in circles with two fingernails. She coughed and cringed, retasting Tanqueray. I left.

"Good-bye," I said, clicking off her light.

"But I don't even know your name!"

I pulled her apartment door locked behind me.

5.

I stopped looking for trouble since I wasn't good at finding it. Conveniently, trouble moved in next door.

6.

It's the Seventh Commandment.

And given that Susan—which isn't a letter close to her real name—was, in fact, my neighbor's wife, the trespass was a little too literal for comfort. In the weaker moments, when she was looking at me without blinking for a dozen seconds, I tried to convince myself that this would be her problem and my nursing-home smile.

"You're easy to talk to," she said, her hazel eyes bigger than satellite dishes. We were standing in my kitchen on a Saturday morning, having coffee. As usual, she stopped by after her bagel run. Over about four months in 2002, we'd sidled into a fondness for each other mainly fueled by our living about seventeen feet apart. On this Saturday morning, Susan's collarbone poked atop her blue sleep shirt, her hair was banded back except for the blond wisps that fell on her neck. She sipped her coffee. She was the sweet, flawless wife that men fantasize about capturing. The hitch was that the young heart-drug salesman next door didn't need to fantasize.

Still, I sensed Susan would slip into my arms easier than a moth-chewed cardigan.

Standing at my fridge, at 9:49 A.M., the TV's chatter in the background, I felt her pulling me to her like lint to a black hole. Just one goddamned kiss . . . I started mentally drawing Clarence Darrow diagrams of ethics and culpability. I smelled her lavender body wash. At any moment my sway could have become a lean.

She was perfect, and perfectly out of the question.

Six times I've found perfection in another man's woman.

The gravest were imagined and never tested, which is why I don't own a gun. The comfort and proximity you have to a pal's girlfriend, the flow you feel with a married bar mate . . . it's a chemical sanctuary. It breeds an easiness that melts the biological caution we maintain when we smell quarry. Like two cannibals meeting on full stomachs. Nothing bonds two unpairable people like the innocent tension of a conspiratorial, unspoken "if only."

Compassion, shame, fear of consequences—they're mast lines of morality. And Susan, by poking around my door with a one-and-a-half-carat ring and a gentle heart, gentler than any woman I've met, was a forming gale.

7.

She never spoke directly of her husband, Art. Only logistically—we went to this restaurant, he's in Seattle, he is not home. He frequently passed me in the hall and smiled broadly, sometimes apologizing for their cat sneaking into my apartment when it escaped into the hallway—which it did every day—whenever I happened to be coming or going. I wavered between wanting to embrace him as an envied, unknowing brother who stumbled into paradise by snagging a wife like Susan, and wanting to snap his spine on my knee and stuff him down the trash chute. Not to eliminate him as a barrier to Susan. But for a darker motivation. One that's difficult to describe.

Sicilians call it the *cornuto*. The man whose wife could, would, or did cheat on him. He's lower than anything alive, a shamed pariah, a walking dead man who can't be further

emasculated. As such, he has obligations that must be tolerated. Like killing his wife, the man she slept with, and a good
part of the village and several chickens for measure. In 1995,
in a sweltering snack-bar in Sicily, I remember an elderly man
shaking his head over the talk of a double homicide trial. The
killer got nine years. The old man was surprised at the sever-
ity of the sentence. I asked why.

He covertly made the horns with his wrinkled hand.
"Cornuto," he whispered so I could barely hear him.

8.

Susan walked through my door at 10:30 P.M. that same
Saturday night, the cat slung in her elbow. She was wearing
the cut sweatpants, the ones that danced just above her meaty
midwestern cheerleader thighs. Her skin shined like jelly. I
somehow sensed that the faintest fur anywhere on her body
would likely be a few loose hairs from the fat animal at her
hip. To say I wanted her would be like saying something that
was very understated.

"Want to see something incredible?" she asked.

"I probably ought not to," I said.

She laid the cat prone and stroked its stomach. It fell asleep
like a crocodile.

"Poor fixed son of a bitch," I muttered. I imagined it and
Art playing mattress bookends to her.

Susan began casually straightening the framed newspapers
I pretend are paintings. Blood gushed below my belt. I envisioned touching her warm arms and guiding her into the room
at the right. For God's sake, wouldn't it satisfy the impatient

law of nature? Only a man-made convention, an idea, disliked the urge; some Lincoln notion about not smashing down another man's house so you can sleep soundly in yours. Some quaint rule that's broken six trillion times a second, and that's in Nevada alone.

I noted the small catch-22: if this angelic girl I longed to wake up next to actually ever woke up next to me, I might get the queasy impulse to count the cash in my wallet and kick her out. Groucho was on to something.

I examined the fourteen-pound dust mop sleeping on my couch. Then I watched Susan squint to read the old mailing label on a *Life* under glass. I couldn't tell her to go away, and I couldn't have her. I felt frozen between trip wires. The way forward or back seemed equally treacherous. But I'd have to go one way. And she had all the power here; as decent a man I like to pretend I am, if she came within a breath of me, touched me some way, in any way, and unseamed her mouth, thinking would be over, and my tongue would have slipped into her as easily and gently as our fingers slipping together. Whichever way I inched, she had all the power. I was free. She was not.

She and Art are still married. She told me marriage was complicated. So complicated.

More than Art will know, I suppose.

I deeply wished that I had met her earlier.

But if I had met her earlier, would she have been someone else?

CHAPTER FOURTEEN

Enter the Matchmaker

1.

Seek professional help.

It's a recommendation we hear often. Some people hear it more often than others.

And it amply applies to dating and sex now—and all the practitioners aren't in thigh-high boots and thick makeup. Many of the consultants focus on making you more datable. My first venture into getting some grooming so I might make a groom came in the spring of 2002. I met a "dating coach."

There are thousands of dating coaches operating in the U.S., but I was skeptical of her ability to give me any useful guidance, since my history with coaches of all kinds has been spotty.

For example, I vividly remember my baseball coach pulling me aside before a clutch at-bat, twenty years ago. He raised an index finger and spoke in hoarse, slow blarney: "Get dirty, no thinking, and don't slop up the ball with your Italian grease."

That was his guidance.

Still, he was the coach, so I absorbed his words like an en-tranced soldier. The rest is fuzzy now; I either doubled to cen-ter or missed three thirty-eight-mph pitches. Considering that my coach was a fifty-three-year-old guy who taught typ-ing and cracked weenie jokes, I decided that the person I sought to help strategize my dating life would be an altogether different human being.

One with smaller breasts, hopefully.

I caught a CBS talk show. It billed Leslie Karsner as a "ro-mance coach" with hundreds of clients—mostly men with de-cent salaries and empty beds. For eighty-five dollars an hour, she gives them pointers and counseling to fill the latter. She was pretty. I arranged a session with her.

We met in a Washington, D.C. hotel lounge. She's blond, bright-smiled, and lithe, about thirty-six. Her violet eye shadow matched her pants. As we started, I had an irresistible notion: one of the hot, popular girls from high school was finally giv-ing me a private sit-down to itemize the form-tweaks I needed to get into her Candies. I licked a pen.

"You . . . are a gentleman," Leslie commenced. "That's a turn-on."

I scribbled this down.

"What's your relationship goal?"

The asinine simplicity of the question made me blink; I searched for a young couple tonguing in a dark corner. I ut-tered something about marriage.

She was sweetly off and rolling. "Love is action," she em-phasized at some point. "For instance, when did you last meet a woman who interested you?" Four days before, I replied.

She was singing Billie Holiday songs in Arturro's, and we exchanged cards. Leslie grimaced.

"Why didn't you call her the day after you met her?"

"Can't do that." I shook. "Overeager."

"Always call the day after," Leslie countered. "That's when her enthusiasm is highest, so it's your best shot."

I doubted this, but the coach's vagina was incontrovertible. I wrote this advice down.

Next came Leslie's "Four Pillars of Romance" test. I scored brilliantly in the Vitality and Passion departments. "Lust for the moment, sentimentality, love of fine things . . . those are your definite strengths," she purred. "Right-o," I replied, spying her naked ring finger. Then I tanked on Magic and Comfort.

"Do you ever let your inner child out to play?" she asked, hoping to spot me a charity point for spontaneity. "Not since he whizzed on the carpet," I said. I needed extensive work on pillow talk and long, lovey mind melds, she noted.

The meter running, I skipped to the salient: my looks.

She inhaled awkwardly at this chestnut. After I squashed her gentle evasions, she described what women see across the tablecloth.

"Your facial expression is far too serious," she said. "You're looking at me through the top of your glasses . . . it's harsh, interrogative." Then she flagged the bear-eating-sandwich posture I strike to connote interest. "Don't hunch forward; it's tense. Sit back! Drop your shoulders, let a forearm dangle. Make your body language more sexually exciting. Besides, hunching brings out your double chin."

Ouch. That inspired a query. "You could be in . . . better shape," she replied gingerly. "Tone is what we want."

I felt my testicles ascend.

She scanned my rat-bit fingers ("Get a manicure") and then my lace-ups. "Shoes are the defining point," she lectured. "Never let a woman you're interested in see you in less than perfect shoes."

Things brightened: she praised my sense of humor.

"Your chuckle is sexy," she granted. "You remind me of Jason Alexander . . . but you don't have his self-assuredness. Your hesitation about how you look stunts your sexiness. Women pick up on it immediately."

George Costanza, but less manly. I had beckoned her size-four stiletto so far up my butt there was no escaping the coup de grâce.

"Leslie, first impressions . . . am I a man you'd want to sleep with or just a nice guy?"

She looked at me with anguished pleas, like a tobacco exec forced to compliment someone's tracheotomy.

"Lay it out," I said, swallowing.

". . . A nice guy. But that's not bad! That's not—"

I scribbled this angrily. She kept talking. She was sweet as fig pie, but I had pressed for candor. I wanted to machine-gun the lounge, napalm the city, and crash my car at 140 mph through a Cracker Barrel store. Professional hot-girl verdict: I'm motherfucking Barney.

2.

I appreciated Leslie's input and wrote it up and tried to forget about it, though I did hit the gym once more every week, for two weeks.

3.

The romance coach had only provided a little coaching. If I'm going to part with money to seek an expert, why not find one who'll provide coaching and a woman to run drills on?

Two months after I sat with Leslie, *Men's Health* presented me with just that opportunity. They were going to pair me up with a professional matchmaker. Her name was Janis Spindel, and she's been a professional matchmaker in the broken-heart capital of the world since the early nineties.

I sat across from her in Patsy's during our initial dinner meeting. She's a skinny brunette, fiftyish, Type A, ambitious and hard-boiled with urban moxie, the end of her every syllable thinned to a razor that cuts your eardrums.

The hordes of desperate, well-paid singles who moan into their drinks in Manhattan have made Spindel—who operates under a business named Serious Matchmaking, Inc.—both rich and seemingly authoritative. She's waxed romantic on television talk shows, and been profiled in a stack of newspaper feature stories touting what's described as her luxury service. In person, she's the sharp-witted, million-watt-personality yenta who attracts swarms of perfumed socialites hungry to find a husband—and she has enough chutzpah to sell ice cubes to an Eskimo.

Spindel's offering isn't akin to Match.com. Or a singles group that'll set you up on lunch dates for a few hundred bucks. She's pricey. She wants fifteen thousand dollars to set you up with twelve women in one year. Fees can go up to twenty-five thousand dollars or fifty thousand dollars or much more, for extra services like teaching you how to act, look, and smell like a marriageable man.

Who would be fool enough to pay this kind of money for a blind-date go-between? Spindel claims she currently has more than seven hundred active clients (90 percent of whom are male). She also boasts a contact list of more than four thousand women, and the majority of them paid her four hundred dollars for the chance to get into this database.

Results? "I'm responsible for three hundred and seven marriages and six hundred committed relationships," Spindel says.

During that night in Patsy's restaurant, we were on a fake date. She noted my looks and posture, my confidence level, and my ability to play the badminton of male-female repartee. She asked pointed questions. What kind of woman do I like? Which traits are the must-haves? Which are deal breakers?

It was like asking a polar bear what flavor seal he likes best.

I'm a man—I have a billion preferences, and they all usually go to hell the minute I meet a new woman. To play along, I rattled off qualities that have appealed to me: Pretty. Brunette. Smart enough to use her tongue as a scalpel. Able to laugh and nurse children. It was about as helpful as a wanted poster that said *white guy*.

These are my druthers, but not necessarily my options. Spindel mentally appraised the breed of female that I could realistically keep in my bed, based on what I bring to the table. I'm a journalist, not the CEO of a semiconductor company or a successful plumber. If there was a "handsome" scale ranging from Steve Buscemi to George Clooney, I'd have to bribe my way up a few notches to teeter at the halfway mark.

Spindel told me how she does her voodoo. "It's an in-stinct—someone will pop into my head, and I may not even know the reason," she said. "In fact, I already have someone in mind for you."

I snapped to attention like a Jack Russell hearing the can opener.

"And she is cah-yute. But first we need to get you into shape."

4.

Four days later, I had clothes arranged in my place in neat piles, separated by season and function. Spindel's image con-sultant, Elena Castaneda, instructed me to do this before her house call. It was the first light many of these clothes had seen since Dan Quayle jokes were in. They hung around because I had never really perfected the guy who bought them. As long as they were handy, I might still get around to it.

Ding-dong. Castaneda walked in. She's a fit, dark-haired beauty with European features and the light, crisp smell of a classy woman in her late thirties. "Image consultant" has the potential to be a horse-crap title, but actual sartorial knowl-edge can't be easily faked. Castaneda has a fashion degree and experience as a retail-clothing buyer and shop owner.

She completed her appraisal of my apartment in five sec-onds, as a woman can. We all live in giant résumés.

"This place is . . . nice," she said. It took me three minutes to convince her to take off the kid gloves. Some of her clients must be touchy bastards.

"Your place is a bachelor cliché," she affirmed. "No soft

edges, a lot of metal and glass, a lot of black and gray, every-thing sterile and cold."

We locked eyes for a moment. "I'm never getting rid of my black leather couch," I said. "It cleans off with Windex."

She noted the boundary and gave me strict prescriptions: Put carpets on the hardwood floors. Buy softer lighting. Paint over the white walls with any soft color—the bedroom a dif-ferent color than the hall or living room. Make the place warmer and cozier. These orders were positively clear and helpful and I thought, why don't I just pump a bullet in the head of the younger guy who still lives here?

We headed into the bedroom. Her look of dismay was fa-miliar.

"The comforter . . ."

"I got it freshman year," I told her. "It's a trouper!" Aside from my couch, this is my most—"

"Invest in bedding," she said, looking at me as though I could forget anything else she might say in the next hour. "You want to make your bed as inviting as possible because everything leads there." A new silk-cotton comforter, lush blankets, three-hundred-thread-count sheets, throw pillows— I needed them like England needs dentistry.

"And put on a soft headboard," she instructed. Leather or cloth. "Women love soft headboards. You'll see."

I had cleaned my place for her arrival hurriedly, the way you do when there's a chance the visitor might sleep with you. My labors had notched it up to "unkempt."

The peeking refuse from my hurried job wasn't entirely a bad thing, Castaneda told me. "If your place is a little messy, it means she can add her touch. If everything is neatly organized, she'll think, I'll have to fit into his lifestyle—there's no place for me."

"I'm wide open," I said, looking around. She studied me for an instant with a feminine smile. Yes and no, her gaze said.

Still unconvinced she was worth two hundred dollars an hour (Castaneda's usual fee when working with Spindel), I escorted her through my dud heaps. Her frequent command was, "Throw this out."

"Your clothing style is what I'd call 'updated classic,' " she said. My clothes—all my clothes—were ridiculously conservative and stodgy for a thirty-four-year-old single man. Instead of dressing like Humphrey Bogart in 1955, I could keep a few Bogey elements—my dark suits, my best two-button-collar dress shirts, my old watches—and pump in some modern juice. After a grueling hour, I saw the death of many friends that predated my comforter.

The contrary side of me wanted to keep the "thanks, but I know how to dress myself" delusion going. But Castaneda was dead-on. Women have tried to help me in the past; they just didn't have the sense to make me pay enough so that I'd actually listen.

She eyed me for ten seconds.

"Get rid of your glasses or wear softer frames. Your glasses hide your eyes. Women want to see your eyes. You need to lose twenty pounds. You'll carry yourself completely differently, and you'll wear your clothes much better. Have pride in your hairline. You can tell you're self-conscious about it, and that's much worse than having a receding hairline—go get a hairstyle that doesn't hide it."

When she stopped talking, I kept scribbling, wondering when the recommendation for penile enlargement surgery was coming. I looked up.

"We need to see a plastic surgeon," she began. Eight days later, we did.

Meanwhile, Spindel coughed up my first match.

5.

"Her name is Suzie," she said on the phone two days after Castaneda's strategic strike. She was thirty-three, lived in Connecticut, worked in pharmaceuticals.

Calling my prospect was easy. It was like a business trans-action. "Can we meet on Thursday?" I asked, as if I had some brochures I wanted to give her. Come that day, I stood watch at the mouth of the Oyster Bar in Grand Central Station for fifteen minutes after 8:00, eyeing a total of six solo females, my prayers split for and against. Finally, my raised eyebrow found another.

Suzie was pretty. She had brownish blond hair and stood about five-two, with a body between good and rockin'. She had the face of an innocent, let's-eat-s'mores-on-Friday-night girl. Her eyes were so large and so blue you couldn't avert your gaze. They were ocean blue. And big.

"Your eyes are incredibly blue," I declared during dinner as she tenderly forked her whitefish.

"I get that a lot," she said, sweetly. It was match number one, and the woman opposite me inspired the two things that topped my wish list for a future wife: I had the strong urge to have sex with her, and I had the serious notion that I might still be glad to see her in my bed when I opened my eyes eleven minutes later.

The advantages of having a matchmaker were immediately apparent. Spindel was the icebreaker topic, and given her pronounced personality and occupation, there was enough to talk about. Secondly, this wasn't a blind date set up by a cousin or a coworker; if Suzie and I didn't mesh, neither of us would harm our intermediary's feelings, and we'd almost assuredly go peaceably to our deaths without ever meeting again. Finally, the dinner had more gravity than a generic Internet coffee date. A hard-talking, high-end guru of hookups thought we two had romance potential. That gave us more psychic glue than relying on our own faulty judgments.

"So? So?" Spindel pressed, ringing me shortly before midnight. Her phone demeanor had the remarkable sales quality of making you feel as if you were the only person in the world she cared about, and making you happy was her life's mission. Knowing that her calls could also bring a new female made me a receptive receiver.

"I think we hit the jackpot," I replied. It occurred to me that if that were so, Spindel would have pocketed an obscene wad faster than an Enron exec. Being a Realtor to the homeless must be a sweet gig sometimes.

"Suzie's terrific," I continued, "but my male intuition tells me that she wants a low-key, stay-at-home guy who will get married soon and give her a safe, reliable life." I paused to think where exactly the negatives were in this. "I don't see her building a relationship with me if I'm not going to be that guy."

"Your male intuition is wrong," Spindel replied.

"What did Suzie say about the date?" I asked, another advantage of having a high-priced matchmaker.

"She didn't really say anything negative. . . . She had a good time," Spindel answered. My bullshit alarm rang, which instantly snuffed my ego glow. Fuckin' figures, I thought. Spindel wouldn't spill any other details. She just recommended a second date with Suzie.

"Can we continue to scout as well?" I asked. "I'm not getting any younger."

6.

For match number two, Spindel served up Ariel, an athletically built twenty-seven-year-old with brown hair and a pretty, tomboyish face. We met at a fancy Chinese restaurant for a long lunch. I couldn't determine whether Ariel's casualness was the mark of a brilliantly laid-back girl or a lack of interest in me. Naturally, I assumed the first. Ariel said she was a novelist and was constantly traveling, and vague details led me to suspect a trust fund was in the picture. An hour later, on the corner of Forty-eighth and Third, she hugged me quickly as if I were her nephew. She's shy, I thought. Adorable. I figured I'd call her tomorrow to make plans for date two, and then decide whether to treat Suzie to Wendy's or Mickey D's should our plans hold.

"It wasn't really happening for her," Spindel said the next day.

I waited for the punch line.

I can get crapped on by women without your help, I

thought. Suffering two teeth-kickings by women a high-paid matchmaker brought to me isn't my idea of luxury service.

"Anything specific?" I ventured, like an employee wanting to know why he was canned. But again, Spindel was conciliatory—"the women who don't work out can give me a clearer idea of who's right for you"—but she wouldn't elaborate. This was probably good for me, I realized later. If you give too much legitimacy to any opinion that makes you view your intrinsic traits—like height, looks, inclinations, or knob size—as flaws, you'll start brandishing yourself as a loser. I've known several people with this disease. Of both sexes. As I've mentioned, I believe God plants them around to serve as warnings.

7.

A few days later, I had the rematch with Suzie at the venerable downtown Italian joint Il Buco. She looked delectable, which disarmed my ire about her tepid rating of our previous date. Three white-haired dons at the next table discussed her virtues in an Italian dialect over their sangria, an occurrence as natural as a dog licking himself. She noticed their conspiratorial glances.

"They like your blue eyes," I lied.

"You two are married?" the closest sixtyish man asked.

"It's our second date," Suzie answered.

He made an expression of perplexed disapproval. "For when you are married," he said, raising his glass. His two cronies followed suit. Suzie laughed, I laughed, we reciprocated. And within minutes I assumed they had cursed the evening.

For the next two hours, Suzie said next to nothing. It was

like trying to pull conversation out of a painting. It sucked
hard. By the time the tiramisu came I was ready to punt. I've
witnessed the second-date reversal many times, I reminded
myself. The second date often blows because, in most instances, it's actually the real first date. If she's nice to look at,
the anticipation and newness of the first-first date can provide an espresso shot of stimulation that keeps you entertained through the first hour. The canned introductory stories
about middle-name origins and roommate tics can provide
amusement for an hour. But the follow-up date? Most of the
superficial details and polished opening bits have been spent,
and the diversion of newness has thinned. Realness gets a
chance to peek out. Anticipation has begun to meld into expectation. And a woman can look, smell, talk, and feel dis-
turbingly different than she did seventy-two hours before. It
happens. Sometimes it's mutual.

"She had the best time!" Spindel said. "She couldn't stop
talking about her evening with you."

"I don't think we were on the same date," I replied. "She
didn't say two words in two hours. I'm not into it."

"That's . . . interesting," Spindel said. "We need a third
date."

I was silent.

"I'll talk to her," she said dutifully.

8.

The following Thursday, I sat in the plush office of a well-
known plastic surgeon in the city that doesn't get beauty
sleep.

"We need to get rid of this double chin," Castaneda said, pointing to my facial love handles.

"We'll do liposuction with a small incision under the chin," the doctor said, examining me. He explained the deal: local anesthesia, a couple of days with my head wrapped toothache-style, a week's healing, and wham—a stronger jawline. I'd go from Flounder in *Animal House* to Dick Tracy in an hour.

"It would make a big difference," Castaneda assured me. I slowly nodded, pinching the neck swaggle I clearly hadn't realized was so ruinous to my life. I was one year of dinners away from Oliver Hardy.

"How much?" I asked.

Only 2,800 dollars. Pennies for a man who procures the services of a matchmaker.

9.

One-on-one matchmaking is only one of Spindel's offerings; she throws matchup dinners and large parties, too. I attended a few, and during one hotel shindig I had Betsy, a thirty-three-year-old coworker, in tow. She's a kindhearted Texan stunner any guy would love to whisk to a Vegas chapel in a blink were it not for her happy marriage to a lucky guy.

The party gave me a clearer idea of Spindel's clientele, though it was impossible to tell who was a client, a prospect, a flunky, or a come-with, like Betsy. Spindel had mentioned to me that she didn't take on men who were fat, short, poor, or "schlubs." If I'm not the perfect storm in that equation, I'm not missing by much. But by the looks of the other male attendees, there may be more wiggle room than I suspected. Dozens of—forgive me, Jesus—objectively homely men ranging in age from their forties to their sixties milled about the room searching for face time with women dressed to the aces. We struck up conversations with accountants, bankers, technology geeks, owners of chain-store empires, and Wall Street types, many in expensive suits and velvet-box watches that hinted at a booming career but—given the many faltering attempts at flirting—a bereft love life.

In the span of two hours, the flickering remains of one of the most hopeful myths I've held since childhood was destroyed. I encountered men in the room who had kicked the living hell out of life in critical areas that matter. They had achieved prestige and power in their industries. They had accumulated wealth. They were sharp and out of their thirties, with enough life training to chuckle at trivialities and petty fears that harangue younger men—one would think. But when approaching a woman, or wanting to, several of these men took on the pleading eyes of an adolescent, the nervous mannerisms and pained self-consciousness of a teen at a dance.

Some notion I learned early offered the assurance that conquering material challenges in life—attaining maturity, wisdom and more than twenty-seven dollars in the bank—would eliminate these defects as a natural matter of course. I know no man conquers these impulses completely, but I still followed the carrot of that assumption. These guys were living refutations of it. They were a contradiction I couldn't rectify: they could swim the English Channel but couldn't tread water. I still had all my effort funneled into making good. I never had the serious thought that a mentally functional man might not ripen uniformly. The possibility of being an outwardly successful man-child ten years from now, but still inwardly fearful around beautiful women, made me want to shit my boxers.

As for the women, most of the gals were in their forties or better and looked as if they had a nose for, or were acclimatized to, money. Spindel and her pretty assistants (who have assumed the pose of would-be clients in some newspaper photos) interviewed each one as she entered the door, marking on clipboards their relationship status, occupation, education, weight, height, and other vitals. Average-looking women were sometimes let through without undergoing this; attractive women received longer interrogations. They'd be likely candidates for Spindel's four-hundred-dollar thirty-minute session. Betsy, my coworker there for kicks, was jumped on by a clipboard wielder.

At least one partygoer seconded the assistant's taste. An hour into the event, while she was standing placidly, Betsy's eyes enlarged.

"What's the matter?" I asked.

"That man just pinched my butt really hard," she said, wincing, her face contorting in pain. I turned angrily to see a frail, bald, doddering man with a mischievous grin slowly disappear into the single bodies, heading for parts unknown.

10.

Match number three was Chloe, a thirty-five-year-old publishing executive who had sixty people reporting to her but zero reporting to her bedchamber. We met at Matt's Grill for a bite after work. She was nice-looking, but would be an undisputed hottie with more feminine touches in her hairstyle. (It was blond, short, and bundled—all business.)

Chloe was a harried career chick who was beginning to panic about her unborn children. She wanted a serious relationship, marriage, but she had momentum in her job. Stopping now would undo years of work, she said. She was too entrenched, achieving too much. Dollars and new responsibilities were flying in. We both sipped our drinks; the colossal drawback to her argument made its lone point during the silence.

Men are intimidated by high-achieving women, Chloe added. They run, searching for partners they can handle. I've heard untold numbers of women say this, but it's only half the story. Just as women look for a man who'll be a decent father, men outside of their twenties—or whenever their brain and their dick begin to function independently—also judge women on their mothering quotient. At least I have. Parenthood requires a certain divestiture of other ambitions for upwards of a decade, if not permanently. The more alien I think this concept is going to be to a woman—i.e., her kid will be one slice in her pie rather than the whole crust, fruit, and sugar sprinkles—the less comfortable I feel about jumping off the parenthood cliff with her. If you're marrying June Lockhart, you know the kids will be all right. Join forces with Martha Stewart and it gets iffy.

"Will I hear from you again?" Chloe said suspiciously as I opened her cab door.

"Yes," I said, weirded by her suspicion. She did, the next day.

The day after that she was off to her Berlin office for a month, then to the West Coast for some days or weeks after that. And so on, as time melted into frequent-flier miles. In her pie, I wasn't even a crumb. I like to think she'll stop when she's ready, or she'll meet a man who can keep her grounded. Given that I'm uncertain how ready I am, even if she chipped a spark for me, I couldn't be that guy. It's hard to argue the merits of conviction if your own isn't solid.

11.

"You're having crappy luck, aren't you?" Spindel said. "A lot of my clients have success after three matches. Most are in a committed relationship within ninety days."

"Crappy luck?" I repeated back. With just these three particular girls? She was insinuating I was the stick in the spokes here. Which I was, I suppose, somehow. While I badly wanted to meet that woman who blinds me to all others, I realized that I had a slight fear that this matchmaker experiment might actually be successful—successful but still fall short of that immature ideal. What then? I like the concept of marriage, always have, but the inner-guts reality of it is as mysterious to me as the contents of pork sausage. Like many men in their thirties, I have a strong force pulling me forward and a weaker force beckoning me back. The notion of settling down, or emptying a vacation fund to buy reflective lighting, releases the hand brake. This fear is always in the mix when dating starts involving the *us* talk. Maybe it's there at the outset, too. The artificiality of being formally paired with women I knew up front had serious intentions forced me to confront this.

There was another disadvantage to my journalistic test-drive of Spindel's service. I wasn't paying full boat, and that left me with only the motivation of a regular guy who wants to find a woman to date and end his loneliness, rather than the frustrated urgency of a man who just shelled out ten thousand dollars or more and has a dwindling number of at-bats with each miss. Paying a ridiculous price for something makes you value it more. Look at Iraq.

"I can bring the horse to water, but I can't make him drink," Spindel said, referring to my fickleness with Suzie and inability to wow the panties off Ariel. "You know, match-making takes a great deal of effort and time."

I felt like apologizing for not having proposed to Suzie yet, or having hopped a jet to Spain and kidnapped Chloe out of a board meeting. It was an interesting trap; a matchmaker is really beyond culpability for a setup gone awry, because a desperate guy's ability to disappoint a woman has no bottom. By the time men are old enough to afford a ten-thousand-dollar fee, they've had enough conditioning with female failures to accept blame without question.

Not everyone, though. Spindel, like any other business owner, has been sued by disgruntled clients. For all those who publicly glow about her service, she also has her fair share of unhappy alumni.

Whether any matchmaker, or any force of nature, could have secured mates for some of these people is up for debate. In helping many singles write their online dating profiles— occasionally letting them know that they are actually seeking the advice of an unmarried man who is currently out of clean laundry and almost certainly masturbates more than they do—I've seen plenty of people with delusional ambitions. (Aside from the one in my bathroom mirror.) I always give these folks wide berth, as the point at which irrational aspirations stop and mental illness begins can be fuzzy.

12.

Match number four made God weep.

"I have no idea why she thought I would get along with you," Allessandra said, poking at her teriyaki stir-fry with palpable disgust. She was a brown-haired babe compressed into a five-four package, who would have been gorgeous had she had one likable atom in her body.

"For God's sakes, I'm looking for a jet-setter—someone to help me in my career and wine and dine me in expensive places. I mean, I'm sorry, but I hate this place."

"It's my local," I said. "They just got a new sixty-four-inch TV."

"I can't believe she told you I was 'down-to-earth,'" she continued, chuckling at the rafters. "I'm the exact opposite of down-to-earth! I actually told her specifically to please not ever send me on a date with a man she thinks is down-to-earth."

We weren't going back to my place.

"So?" Spindel pressed. "She was cah-yute, huh?"

I smacked my lips. I said much, but ended with, "Anybody who has ever talked to me for two minutes would not have put me in the same room with her."

"That's very . . . interesting," Spindel said after a long second. I speculated that she had thrown in a long shot to see if she might get lucky, and Allessandra was a sweet-looking chick. I was also mollified due to a call from Suzie; she had awkwardly worked into our conversation several times how nervous she was at the Italian restaurant, "which may have been wrongly perceived as her being disinterested." It was an endearing call. Both high-schoolish and bluntly adult. She wasn't the type of woman I envisioned seducing with an eye toward marriage. But if she was a near-fit, would I regret ducking her?

13.

The day came for me to make a follow up appointment to have my chin fat sucked out. I looked in the mirror for thirty minutes. I'm no stranger to the scalpel: I had my nose fixed after a car accident in '88, hair plugs filled in a scar from said accident shortly thereafter, and my tits were snipped off due to my aforementioned gynecomastia in my twenties. But those all had some underlying reason . . . if only to stop whistles from nearsighted construction men.

The chin was not that.

Not yet, I decided. That road is for somebody else, at least now. If I'm going to turn myself into a Phyllis Diller, the first domino isn't falling at thirty-four.

14.

Match number five. Carrie.

"Okay, now I'm kind of starting to think you're just throwing stuff at the wall and seeing what sticks," I said to Spindel later, sweating a bit. "Carrie's a marathon runner who's looking for an earth-granola boy. Dinner was pretty awkward."

Spindel let out a long sigh. "Elena thought you two would hit it off. I didn't pick her."

Smarting from two train-wreck pairings, and maybe a bit frustrated—having invested effort by now, if not equity—I needed an ego salve. And to answer a lingering question. I dialed Suzie.

"I'm so glad to hear from you," she said, waking up from a nap. "I was thinking of you, and I don't think coincidences are just random."

My initial reservations held, but something about her made me feel good. We had a third date, cut short by her need to catch an early train home. On the fourth date, she reclined on my couch at the end of the evening, her smooth, shining calves across my knees. I slipped a black high heel off and stroked the topside of her perfect girl foot, massaging the nook above her toes with my thumbs as if I knew what I was doing. She smiled at me, a bit languorously due to our long night. Her eyes were a dark navy without the light. The other shoe dropped. I'd move into her in a dozen seconds, but I loved this moment, the electric nervous anticipation of it. I hoped it would never dissipate. That's probably one of my problems.

Suzie and I weren't ideal. But we weren't absurd. If we found more common threads, maybe we'd find something to build on. Maybe that's how the final one begins; a mustard seed of a relationship, instead of the ice ax to the brain I've always been searching for. We'd go on three more dates before deciding to not go forward, since she wasn't leaving Connecticut, and I wasn't leaving the city.

But it was a close enough near-miss to make me think. Different timing might have changed the script with Suzie. I wasn't ready for the house-in-the-burbs life yet, if I'll ever be. But she grazed me.

A broken clock is right twice a day, I reasoned. But Spindel's first gut hunch was not total hooey.

For many thousands of dollars, it would have been sheer genius.

CHAPTER FIFTEEN

Killing the Column

1.

"The column's had a tremendous run, but the new survey says the younger guys want more of 'The Girl Next Door,' Q and A," the *Men's Health* editor said on the phone.

I sat silent, holding the phone. The bomb had just exploded, taking my whole existence and self-identity with it.

". . . . You shot her in a bra," I finally squeaked forth, referencing her photo.

We settled the details, and I set the receiver down. The Girl Next Door. A Q&A—cue-and-ay—column. With questions such as "Why does she moan sometimes and scream other times?" and "Why do girls cry when we break up even if they're dumping us?"

Meanwhile, I was adding to the insights of mankind.

Such indignities few have endured. I felt like I was a freshly dead Elvis seeing Marty Feldman plastered on the cover of *People* magazine.

Forgive them, they know not what they do, I burned.

"I remember most of your columns, but I can't remember even one of The Girl Next Door questions from the last few issues," one editor at the magazine consoled me.

"The guys in the survey remembered it well enough," I said, sighing.

Clouds gathered over the East River. The wheels of vengeance began to turn.

I will have one dozen essays published in *The New Yorker* in the next three months, I decided. I simply needed to think of some things to write about, and then get to know someone at *The New Yorker*, and then find the time to jot down these ditties.

Hey, they have to fill those pages every week, I thought. I might call the editor and e-mail him or her a rough workup, and they'd get it into final page proofs in two or three days. It's not like Woody Allen and Steve Martin, at their ages, could match the output of a man with a vendetta who could even fact-check his own stuff. After reading that Jay McInerney book fifteen years ago, it's not like I trust their fact-checkers anyway.

As long as no other distracting dilemma nosed its way into my life, my scheme was as good as done.

CHAPTER SIXTEEN

Alone Again, Unnaturally

1.

In the way John Lennon noted that life was, roundabout, what happens when you're making plans, I lost my job.

Well, not exactly lost it, but it was going away. In March 2003, AARP shuttered its New York editorial office and laid off the roughly twenty staffers who had worked on *My Generation*. It was a protracted demise. The AARP had killed *My Generation* in August 2002, and allowed the staffers to help the Washington staff put out the remaining pub (*AARP The Magazine*) for seven months. Finally, as we had been long anticipating, the publisher showed up on a spring Tuesday morning (with the HR rep flanking him, always a beautiful sign) and told us we were all gone. Except we'd have ninety more days of work, and then we'd get the severance. Those last eight months with arp were the most extraordinarily charitable demonstration of slow Band-Aid rippage I'd ever seen.

A twist developed within days. The publisher and editor decided to keep two magazine staffers alive in the New York office. I applied for one of the jobs and got it.

In the next three months, I learned the meaning of survivor guilt.

As the June ax date neared, I stopped feeling like I had been chosen to stay and started feeling like I was being left behind. In a haunted ghost town. While everyone was busy making plans and moving on, building the next thing, I wasn't. I had been offered a slot that would keep me in the same office on the same floor of the same building, alone, for an undetermined time. The bosses weren't keen on employees working from home, since a few experiments with that caused cell phones to ring during Pilates classes.

After June 1, 2003, my thirty-third birthday, my life became a cross between *28 Days Later* and *The Shining*.

Every one of twenty-seven empty offices on the abandoned forty-first floor of the skyscraper was left intact. The staffers' nameplates were still on their doors, their unwanted personal effects and scribbled notes strewn and tacked just as they had been for two years. Celestial Seasonings boxes and Chinese takeout mustard and soy sauce packets remained right where they had been.

As did I.

2.

Solitary confinement can change a man. The other remaining staffer was the art director, and he was only in once a week. I had thoughts of riding a tricycle around the hallways and seeing if stopping by any particular office paralyzed me in fright and caused me to drool. I moved into the largest corner office and watched the sunset from its couch. I ate lunch and napped in each corner office, rotating around the forty-first floor counterclockwise. I sat at everyone's desk and tried to mentally channel them, and see what the earth was like from their vantage point. I could sense that they liked to file things. Make piles. Write down phone numbers on Post-Its next to the phone. They stapled and clipped. They listened to the hum of the heating and cooling system quite a bit. They worked in chairs that were adjusted far too low and far too high. They heard someone come in occasionally and wondered who it was and what they wanted, since you needed a magnetic card to open the door, and they would creep toward the doors and snake their head around the reception area with wide eyes, like Gollum from *Lord of the Rings*. Sometimes they slapped their stomachs to make a rhythm for twenty minutes straight. A few yodeled. All wondered why they were there alone. They realized they could make all the color photocopies they wanted, but had nothing worth copying. They would talk like Donald Duck until they could do it perfectly. They would sometimes be startled when their phone rang while they were at their desk, and they would answer it immediately, telling the caller that they were no longer there and had not been for months. They went barefoot. They didn't shave for several days straight, and then they wore the same pants three days in a row.

"I would love having your setup!" some friends on the outside would tell them.

"We should love it, shouldn't we?" they would ask each other. "We can do anything we want. As long we answer a phone and click on a computer during the right times. We could even build a home gym in here. We could build blanket forts and stay here all weekend. We could let friends from other states sleep here, renting out a thirty-thousand-square foot apartment in Midtown Manhattan for the cost of two six-packs per night. Except we wouldn't trust the janitors to keep their mouths shut. Not even for a few twenties, we bet."

These people were losing their minds.

3.

Naturally, I went looking for a bona fide New York shrink.

"You're a fucking drunk," the first guy told me. He was a psychiatrist in my health insurance plan's network.

"Your face is puffy, you're overweight. You look tired. You've got some rosacea. You're a drunk."

He obviously liked the soft approach.

The shrink was a lanky Tim Robbins look-alike, and he sounded like he was in recovery. He spoke like a missionary from the Temperance movement and admitted he lived a life free of alcohol, caffeine, NutraSweet, sucrose, trans fat, butter, and most other deadly substances.

He was a freak. But I couldn't dismiss him entirely. I was drunk three nights out of seven, and buzzed another two.

I quit drinking.

Problems arose immediately. If you've ever laid down the hooch, you find out instantly that your closest, dearest friends only like you because you drink with them.

"Eh . . . Call me when you're off the wagon," one said to me.

"I didn't come out to sit across from that," said another, referring to my nonalcoholic beer. It was doing something offensive to him, evidently. Cut it out, I said to the pint glass when he was in the bathroom.

Drinking is a second job in New York, but in Allentown it was medication. This was dangerous, because you have to drive in Allentown.

This meant everyone I knew, with few exceptions mainly due to age or infirmity, drove drunk.

I don't mean they drove after a beer or two. I mean drunk.

Drunk driving in Allentown was a bit like sledding in the Alaska tundra. You could try to get by some other way, but every other option was an immense pain in the ass.

And everyone sledded.

In most bars, people would have seven wines and they drove home. Young singles. Forty- and fiftysomething married dudes. I myself drove drunk somewhere between two and twenty thousand times, and I was proud of the low offense rate in my peer group. DWIs seemed to be about as prevalent as high school diplomas.

In ruminating on this, I realized that the whole anti–drunk driving campaign, while it's cut down on fatalities, is really ass-backwards. You will never get the drunk drivers off the road so it'll be safe for sober people.

You have to make the road safe for drunk drivers.

That no one has figured this out astonishes me.

Aside from creating drunk lanes on the highway, which you use exclusively if you've had even one beer under penalty of being immediately shot in the head, there should be massive speed bumps every six feet in suburban neighborhoods.

You have no reason to ever go faster than sixteen miles per hour in suburban neighborhoods. The average unfit person can sprint for short distances at eight miles per hour. A speeding horse and buggy might average fourteen. If I said to someone one hundred years ago, "I will present you with a mode of transportation that will take you around a suburban neighborhood at nearly twice the top speed you can run, would you ever have cause to bitch about that? No, that's right."

Secondly, the design of the automobile is fantastically asinine. Hooking up a gas motor to a metal or wooden frame with wheels was a good experiment, and once it was proven that it could be done it should have been disregarded forever. The same as long-distance ballooning.

If I said to any reasonable human being, "Do you think it's wise to take a two-thousand-pound hard object that can travel at speeds of over one hundred and twenty miles per hour, and allow a single fallible person, at any education level, to have sole judgment and discretion to take this object anywhere he wants at any speed? I will tell you right now that such a thing has been tested for long periods of time, and people smash into themselves and other things at nearly a constant rate, killing thousands of people a day worldwide. Would you think a rational society would say, 'Yes, this is a good idea. Let's do this?' I think not."

Cars should be comprised of two soft spheres with the consistency of gelatin. The occupants remain in the inner sphere, which always stays gravity-side down, and the outer sphere rotates to provide locomotion. If this sphere smacks into any object at up to two hundred miles per hour, it should just flatten to a degree that won't affect the size of the occupant cabin, which will absorb some or redirect all force from the moving occupants to avoid a secondary impact inside, and then the sphere should just bounce away. You end up in a field or floating in a lake or piled on top of sixty other "cars," you shake your head, and go on your way.

Drunk lanes would be eliminated when these soft ball-like cars were perfected, because driving drunk would be harmless. Your sphere would just move erratically, people would know you were drunk, and they'd laugh at you.

Again, what are our best and brightest brains occupying themselves with, when solutions this simple are staring at us with their thumbs in their ears?

I solved this problem and many more while working in the abandoned skyscraper floor on Forty-eighth Street.

4.

The second shrink was a keeper, especially since I was only going to test-drive two. She was not in my health insurance network, which I've forced myself to believe meant she was better. At a rate of one hundred and fifty dollars an hour, she slowly began offering a bevy of interesting suggestions: I'm deathly afraid of taking risks, have a deep fear of being vulnerable, and view females as being out to get me, to name the first three. I began going around town executing her daily experiments (say, talking to any woman wearing red) and repeating three-word, Johnnie Cochran mantras to overcome my relationship neuroses. (Don't isolate, compensate.)

I began to perk up. It's amazing what paying a net of seventy dollars per session after the partial insurance coverage can do to make you feel like you're making progress. I began coping with my isolation, mainly by acts of compensation such as talking to women in red dresses.

I had a hold on sanity once again. Now all I could hope was that nothing would emerge from the bowels of my past to disturb it.

CHAPTER SEVENTEEN

Nicole, Engaged

1.

Thanksgiving. My favorite holiday. It requires gorging and usually no effort on my part. Those are two things I've mastered.

On Thanksgiving night, 2003, Nicole visited my mother's house after dinner, to say hello. There had been no strangeness between us, which I found a marvel. The occasional e-mail or call from her stirred nothing but fondness, a generically warm feeling that one might feel after being contacted by any friend. Of course, there was always the microscopic thought that the latest communication would see, in starkly small letters, *I finally realized that I'm in love with you.*

This is the natural hilt of unspoken anticipation whenever there's a crisp, sealed personally written envelope in your mailbox, or a blinking light on your phone message machine, or an e-mail from an ex or a recent love interest or even an old platonic friend of the opposite sex who had pretty much stopped e-mailing you. Unless you're a stunningly beautiful girl who's the Nicole of many men, or a celebrity being hounded by mentally ill fans, the out-of-the-blue declaration of love via letter, e-mail or phone call is rare. Maybe five to a lifetime, counting the three or four that happen in elementary school. (Unfolding a note from Tammy H. in Mrs. Grimm's class that read *I love you!*, with a confirming wink as she walked away, is my oldest cherished snapshot, circa 1976. And I assumed then that I could rightly expect such notes to come to me in pairs or trios every day or so from that point on, but God dealt me a cruel awakening.)

Even though none of Nicole's notes or calls have ever come close at hinting at a newfound desire for me, I thought it only prudent to prepare myself in the event that did happen. I mentally walked myself through the scenario, creating hypotheticals of what might move her to suddenly feel this way (serious illness, prospect of a long jail sentence that only I could save her from, near-death experience in which some ball of light mentioned me, a strange fortune cookie at a weak moment, or us coincidentally being on the same cruise ship and my saving her from throwing herself off the stern to escape a coerced marriage).

Given the likelihood that at least one if not more of these scenarios would occur, I examined what I would do when confronted with Nicole, wanting to get back into my life. What does any man do when his Nicole wants back in? As I mentioned, Nicoles rarely ever wholeheartedly want in the first time, since they're usually the object of an irrational fixation.

"Why . . . why didn't this happen five years ago?" I only found myself saying to her. No, I wouldn't say that. Good lord, she's distraught, reeling from a near-death experience or facing twenty years in Graterford Prison, and I respond to her by immediately voicing *my* druthers?

Thinking that the utopian situation would give me the opportunity to dismissively snap my fingers in front of Nicole's face was tempting, but it wasn't true. If she were an exgirlfriend of little consequence, a redemptive gesture would be just about all this fantasy would entail. But when a man is actually facing his Nicole, regardless of however ruthlessly he thinks she ripped his gills out at one time, you'd look into her eyes and still be ready to take a Mack truck in the face for her. Sure, you might spend ninety minutes concocting a kiss-off e-mail to a Nicole, far from her, overriding every impulse in your limbic system with the "eat me, bitch" vitriol supplied by your cerebral cortex. You might be curt on the phone, like Jon Favreau at the end of *Swingers*. These are a coward's rebukes, like lobbing a stone instead of punching a chin.

The biological emotions at work with a Nicole, if she was your Nicole, predate telephony and alphabets and probably spoken language. If she's looking at you, you may remember for just a second when you actually understood that imbecilic jazz lyric that goes, "I'd rather be miserable with you than happy with somebody else." The fact that you don't feel this way any longer is irrelevant, since it's not a sane thought. The fact that you felt this way solely due to indignation of her rejection is also irrelevant.

It's like asking if the barn fire that scarred you was started by a match or a spark.

2.

"Can we go to a diner and get some coffee?" Nicole said to me at about 11:00 P.M.

This was odd.

We drove to a nearby diner and found a booth. Nicole was bothered, fidgeting, looking like a rookie doctor who was nervously stalling before telling a patient that their brain cancer was terminal. She breathed in and out a few times, looking at the pastries behind the counter, and then put both of her hands on the table to compose herself.

I watched with fascination and terror. We had talked very little in the previous two years, and had nothing much to do with one another except positive thoughts from afar. I couldn't think of one thing that would cause her to be nervous with me, unless it was such a catastrophic situation that she'd be nervous in revealing it to anyone. But still, why the private audience? This was strange.

She sipped her cocoa, then recomposed her hands.

"I have something to tell you," she said. She elided the *you* a bit to signal it was something regretful, which was already obvious due to her quietly negative, anxious manner.

I had two heavy seconds to contemplate what might come out of her mouth, and what might come out of mine. *Why didn't you tell me this five years ago?* was readied in my throat, though it had always known it would never see the glory of broadcast.

She leaned over and opened her purse, directly opened a specific pocket, and her hands moved together, doing something.

The left one. She held it at her chest, hiding it with her right hand, and then put both hands on the table. She opened the left hand and laid it flat, so I had a full second to examine it. Then she wrung her hands gently together.

These motions seemed to take a long, slow minute, then seemed way too fast, like they happened in the three seconds in which they did. I saw the diamond. I saw it five hundred times in those three seconds,.

"I'm engaged," I think she said. I was still looking at her left hand. I'm big on hands. Nicole has beautiful hands. I suddenly saw that hand tousling my child's hair. Our kid's hair. A boy. The hair was blond, as he was a toddler, but I knew that later it would turn dark like hers. That hand was a mother's hand. I had never imagined that boy before, never, but there was the back of his head, and I loved him so much I was ready to crush the world into cinders for him, and there she was tousling his blondish-brown hair with her left hand. And in the same two seconds I had imagined him for the first time, he was aborted. Not there. Gone. She was there, he was gone. I felt the instant urge to scream for him, like I was trapped behind a glass wall. I mourned for a dead son. Then that was it. These long seconds were over, and she was talking.

"I was afraid to tell you, I just . . . I didn't know if you'd be mad," she said.

I looked at her brown eyes, then back at her hand, still shaken from what I had thought I had just seen, which was too bizarre to contemplate. It was asinine, in that it was so long after the fact, so out of nowhere, and a residual that came from no fantasy nor concoction of images I could remember.

"Why on earth would you think I would be mad?" I responded. I found myself feeling a small but genuine sense of being peeved as I said this, as if she was insinuating that I must be still carrying such a heavy torch for her, or so fragile in the light of any news of her love life, that I would naturally be destroyed by this development or so out-of-my-head crazy that I'd become enraged at her, without any rationale for it, perhaps in the way I had seven years earlier. *I appreciate you're being so sensitive in the way you're breaking this to me, but we're in our mid-thirties now, and I hope you can believe that I feel nothing but happiness for you,* I wanted to say. This was starkly true, the feeling of a kind of happiness for her. Seeing an engagement ring on her was proper, fitting, and long enough in coming for someone who wanted children. Her becoming engaged was inevitable, though it was so long in happening that I began to fear it was not. Seeing that ring on her finger was like finally seeing clothes on a long naked mannequin in a display window. It doesn't greatly affect you, and you're not sure how the mannequin feels about it, but all the same you're a bit gratified because it's the way it ought to be.

"Nicole, I'm happy for you," I said, realizing that being genuinely happy that a good thing had happened to her wasn't exactly being overly generous or gentlemanly. This was her life, her good fortune, and the event made hundreds of riptides other than the few that might break my way.

"Ron, I had to go with my heart," she said, seeming to have anticipated a need to say much more. "If you don't feel something for someone . . ."

"Nicole, half my heart is breaking," I said to her, stopping her from pouring out a useless explanation, hearing the radio therapist trying like hell to tap through. "If you ever need me, you know I'll always feel the same way about you."

"I know," she replied quietly, perhaps thinking this had been harder or easier than she projected, I don't know which. She seemed both sorry and grateful. I felt sorry and grateful, too, which made no sense. I felt no anguish in this, which bothered me. *This must mean more*, I wracked. I remembered Tom Hanks in that scene near the end of *Cast Away*, after his party when the guests were gone. He picks up that fat crab claw from the buffet and drops it, still a walking skeleton but not hungry. He clicks the candle lighter on and off, on and off, making flame effortlessly. Everything around him mocks what he had once endured.

How desperately I once could have used a thimble of detachment from her.

That child didn't have a name. What was his name? I still hate that I don't know.

CHAPTER EIGHTEEN

To the Moon, Alice

1.

"Men are on a trapeze when they're trying to get over a lost love," a psychologist once told me. "No matter how far they go, they keep swinging back to that one girl until they grab onto the next trapeze and let go of her," she explained.

"Your gender might say to 'get over someone, get under someone,'" I replied.

"It's a good saying, but men need a new love more than women do to move on," she said.

In the weeks after Nicole's engagement, I contemplated the cruel simplicity of this cure. So simple. It was like a surgeon cutting your diseased heart out of your chest and holding it in front of you, and saying, "Now all you need is a new one and you'll be fine."

What if it just doesn't happen for me? I began to think. I strained to avoid conjuring that same tired vision of horror in which I'm shuffling along the streets with soiled pants, watching mothers pull their children close and cover their eyes as I touch myself. I envisioned me living exactly as I do now, except with nineteen gray hairs coiled atop my head and a turkey neck that could produce several pairs of moccasins.

Maybe it wouldn't be the worst existence any human has known. I could still eat and drink to my heart's satisfaction, which meant switching my mental image to a wider screen to fit my 320-pound body. I could still volunteer and mentor. Assuming at some point I had started doing either. I could travel the globe to the widest extent my Social Security check allowed. I might live on Mars.

That isn't "then," I told myself, realizing this was actually true. This isn't some alternative universe that congeals into existence after I've decided to cross through a time-warping worm hole.

It's now. Just later.

I wrote that down on a five-by-seven card and posted it on my fridge with an Elvis magnet.

It was quite reassuring, actually. With this realization, I could stop worrying about preventing my life from becoming some squalid, forsaken scene of fetid subsistence.

I was already there!

2.

Armed with this optimism, I began shaking the bushes anew. As 34 closed in, I had a brief affair with a Freudian psychotherapist figure skater who I met on the Internet.

"I don't get 'jokes,'" she said to me in the Columbus Circle subway tunnel after our third date.

"That's okay," I laughed. *I just want to have sex with you.*

For once, I saw nothing whatsoever wrong with this.

Thank you, Doctor.

3.

"Hi Ron, it's Nicole," her voice said through my answering machine. "It's Sunday the twenty seventh, my wedding day."

I grabbed the receiver.

I had left her a well-wishing phone message earlier that morning and she was calling me back.

"Nicole, I hope you have the greatest day of your life," I said.

"You're really sweet to call," she said.

There was not the slightest mention of a "wish you were here" or "wish I was there," since me standing there watching Nicole approach that priest or rabbi, I forget which, would've felt more perverse than having the President attend a ceremonial burning of the White House. I wouldn't come within one hundred and thirty miles of her that day. It was perhaps one of the few weddings in the history of the earth in which a person who was purposely not invited was wholly relieved and gratified to not be invited, while the intermingling feelings between both parties were positive.

I'd throw myself in front of a speeding metro liner for Nicole, but I wouldn't have stepped foot in that church or synagogue to save her life.

We both knew it, and it was the way it ought to be.

I spent the day pushing dead lead in the gym on Fifty-Fourth Street, watching a foreign movie with a load of popcorn, and drinking. Which is to say it was a Sunday.

The groom may have also had something invested in that day in February, 2005. If given the option, he might not have wanted me to be there, as well as any other relics of her past.

Or maybe he wouldn't have given a shit.

4.

"Relocate Geraci to Washington office," the memo read.

It sat on the top of a copier, forgotten, blaring its "CONFIDENTIAL" heading with deafening futility.

Relocate me to Washington. Fire two other employees. Downgrade this person. Promote that person. Reshuffle this department. Reorganize that department. Nine little asterisks spelling initiatives to be carried out, or discussed further, in the next sixty days.

Right now, I imagined, some executive at AARP was wondering where the frig they put that confidential memo.

Or maybe they hired Karl Rove to beef up their internal corporate security.

Mission one was to shred the thing in the slim hopes that one of the two employees designated for the chopping block had not already swung by the copier room that morning and were now sliding their credit card across the counter of a nearby gun store.

Mission two was to buy a goddamned New York apartment before they presented me with a one-way Amtrak ticket, as flattered as I was to be considered worthy by my superiors of the exorbitant cost of relocation.

Why? My cerebral cortex asked. My reaction was immediate and irresolute, and I had no real disdain of D.C. nor AARP—both treated me well, though the former almost mugged me on an abandoned street near Chinatown one dark night about a year prior.

Because you want to start your life, my subconscious replied.

And what the hell does that mean? I countered.

You've been transient since you were 17, idiot. You've never expected to stay in one place for more than a couple years. We're sick of transience. We're sick of hoping for the next thing. We're sick of looking ahead but never making a life. We're sick of buying day passes when it seems like everyone else is signing up for a season. Unpack. It's overdue. Grow something before you leave. You're where we want to be and you're just getting your legs.

Grow something before you leave.

That's the difference between dating and looking for a woman. It's the bedrock under the perfectly sound screw and-impregnate prime directive, a bedrock that remains steadfast even when that directive defies all contracts of nature by, somehow, losing the tiniest smidge of its urgency.

Christ on the cross, I shuddered. *Have I just admitted that I'm officially one millimeter closer to preferring an hour of televised golf over spewing my DNA into the closest cooch?*

No, my subconscious shook. *You have just admitted that you're almost 35 and your maturational development is just slightly less retarded than it was ten minutes ago.*

If anything ever was worth a steak dinner, that was it.

5.

In the summer of '05, I bought an apartment in Greenwich Village that was about the size of a walk-in closet. I paid $395,000 for it, which roughly translated into $50,000 per square meter of breathable air. I sold everything I had to buy it, and might have had to sell blowjobs on Ninth Avenue if the price had been $397,000.

When the ultimatum came from *AARP The Magazine*, I told my boss the truth. I needed roots. Worse than Alex Hailey. He understood, which, just as when leaving *Men's Health*, made things more difficult. Hostility can be exhilarating in its clarity. Kindness amidst sticky situations tap neurons far north of the brain stem, simultaneously saving them while taxing their talent for complexity.

6.

In 2006, for many single New Yorkers, sending fifty bucks to Match.com every now and then expecting little from it, given your past dances, is about as common as occasionally dropping ten bucks on lottery tickets when you're feeling lucky. It's a goose. Maybe the churn has finally brought in that woman who will be a keeper, instead of a two date waste of cash, a month-long sex romp, or a five or six month near miss at bliss.

Just maybe.

Probably not. Most likely not.

But maybe.

And fifty bucks for three-months dotted with a stream of winks from obese women, regular "I make nice man smile very big" e-mails from Russian prostitutes, and the occasional note from a fairly pretty, fairly normal-seeming, fairly viable girl who lives nine blocks away who, hell, could be a promising prospect . . . that's worth $50 in diversion and anticipation—the tiny stoking of that eternal flame of romantic hope—alone.

Westsider35 was a 35-year-old woman who lived on the Upper West Side (my detective skills are second to none). She had radiant blue eyes—beautiful, they were—in all six of her digital photos.

A good sign.

She listed herself as having a few extra pounds, and she did. Maybe twenty five extra, like me, though I won't pretend to share the same liabilities in being a guy with extra cargo who looks about the same in size 34 jeans as he did seven years ago. She looked like a real 35 year old woman you'd meet without wondering how you'd get her home and get her naked, but the notion might grow stronger the longer you looked at her face and the curves that were ample and feminine. Westsider35 was pretty and knew how to strike a quiet gaze, but was no longer—or maybe she never was—someone's aesthetic idea of the standard-rank hot woman a single guy with options ought to get hard over.

Five years ago, I might have overlooked her.

Now I e-mailed her immediately on reading her self-description.

"You stay classy, Planet Earth," she began. Behind these

words was a cerebral, sharp-humored girl who hated unorigi-
nality and would challenge a guy. Hopefully, she was that girl.
You never know.

She looked like an Alice, with her sweet smile and kind,
feminine lips. Perhaps she was. But she also was clearly someone's Nicole. She was a missed summit for some man, for
more reasons than her photos would indicate.

"What's so great about your Amex Blue card?" I e-mailed
her, citing one of her small jokes.

"Well, Ron, when I flash that Blue, it's like I'm Jay-Z
pulling up in a stretch Hummer to the Ritz Carlton wearing a
Patek Phillipe watch," she responded the next day.

Over dinner in an Irish pub a week later, Janie's face looked
far prettier than her photos revealed. She was as funny and
quick in person as on a laptop.

And, quite importantly, I badly wanted to get into her
shirt.

"I have to say, this has been one of the better dates," she
said, grinning slyly.

"Eh, it's all right," I replied, grinning. She read me.

Janie might pan out.

She might not.

But she wasn't a phantom. And that felt good.

*You might grow something if you're reckless enough to get
mixed up with a woman like this,* I thought. *Then all hope for
something better will be over. You'd better be damned careful.*

We'll be careful, my subconscious said.

Just shut up and pay the bill.

ACKNOWLEDGMENTS

Between you and me, I've always looked a bit askance at the Acknowledgments page in books. I just paid fifteen or twenty bucks for some book, and the writer is wasting an entire page—maybe several pages—giving some sort of protracted Oscar speech in which he thanks dozens of people I do not know, and who have nothing to do with the book's content. I didn't buy the book for that. Can't the writer thank everyone in his life in his own time? Or give monogrammed sterling silver pen and pencil sets to show his appreciation? If the book took him twenty-five years to write, caused the breakup of two of his marriages, and fundamentally changed the way humanity regards itself, okay, one page of acknowledgments is warranted. Otherwise, there's no need for the writer to act like he built the Hoover Dam with a hand trowel. If a public thank-you is really the motivation, why can't the writer take out a full-page ad in the *New York Times* and only burden the populace with the details of his gratitude once? That's far preferable to burdening each and every reader who picks up the book from now until the last copy has disintegrated. Christ, every time I cross a bridge, I don't want my FM radio to be highjacked into giving me a two-minute recording in which the architect thanks the city, the cement supplier, the guys on the dredging crew, the lunch truck driver, his now ex-wife, his fourth grade gym teacher, and his mom all the while cracking little inside jokes. If I want that info, I'll dial the phone number posted near the toll booth.

So, please skip this part if you're like-minded.

I've found that hypocrisy gets easier with practice. The cost of including these pages in the book was about 2.8 cents, which I'll round up to 3 cents, so if you'd like a refund for that amount, just let me know.

My first thanks goes to writer Brian McDonald, a friend I met in Matt's Grill on 55th Street several years ago. He introduced me to his agents, Jane Dystel and Miriam Goderich. They welcomed this book. They're marvelous people, generous with their counsel and genuine in their kindness, the same as those you might meet in a small town in Kentucky just as easily as Manhattan. This book only exists because of their faith and patience and talent, and the gratitude I have for that will be eternal, as any hopeful writer with an aging mom will instantly understand.

I owe a big thank-you to my editor at Kensington Books, John Scognamiglio, a fellow Italian who patiently guided me through this process while, somehow, restraining himself from having a hit put out on me at various points. I'm very grateful to Lydia Stein. The other folks at Kensington who made this book happen have my sincerest appreciation, too. I hope to meet them all personally.

In following the custom of using the Acknowledgments page to show public appreciation to all persons who contributed to the author's life in ways that far transcend any direct activity with his or her book—yes, skip this or act now to get your 3 cent refund—I owe pretty much everything I have, in various degrees and forms, to the following people.

Greg Gutfeld, a guy who kept me from shooting myself in Allentown, and a man of such profuse talent it leaks off willy-nilly to those around him, often to their detriment since you need far more than talent to pull off his life. Many hugely successful writers, editors and media mouths are second-rate Gutfelds. The smart ones appreciate the niche. I do.

Denis Boyles. The peak most writers can ever aspire to is being a second-rate Denis Boyles. The rare ability that requires makes it high compliment rather than a niche to exploit. It would be great to get there before I croak.

Mike Corcoran. A friend who will fight for you, make something happen in your life that's cause for celebration, and then celebrate with you. If you're working in magazines, you probably got your job through him.

Jeff Csatari, the guy who hired me a decade ago.

Tom McGrath, my dating column editor to whom I owe whatever dignity the column allowed me to preserve.

Hugh O'Neill. The classiest man to wield a pen, who always raises the gentleman quotient of any room he enters.

Peter Moore, who fostered and tolerated me beyond any obligation implied in the human experience.

Betsy Carter, Helen Rogan and Ann Powell, who fostered and tolerated me beyond what I deserved as well, and at times I'm sure acquired great empathy for Peter Moore.

Steve Slon, Hugh Delehanty and Nancy Graham of *AARP The Magazine*, for giving me a home for three years, and, well, see above.

Dave Zinczenko and Steve Perrine, for helping me flourish, allowing my dating column to see the light of print, and giving me plenty of good advice enroute. Without them, this book and several of the experiences in it wouldn't have happened. For hate mail, they're reachable at *Men's Health* and *Best Life* magazines, respectively.

Mike Lafavore and Mark Bricklin, who gave magazines for men a new framework to stand on, and me a place to learn. The guys at *Men's Health*, especially Matt Marion, Ted Spiker, Joe Kita, and Duane Swierczynski.

Paul Mauro, who euthanized many cold beers by saying, "Not for nothing, but don't you have a book to write?" Audra Shanley. Christine Reslmaier. Betsy Stephens. Joe Huber. Jessica Frank. Patricia Henry, Liz Irmiter and the guys at the 92nd Street Y and all of the great people who came to my seminars over the years. Jeffery Lindenmuth and his beautiful wife, Terri. Laura Oliff. Steve Erle. Anne Alfaro. Amy Antolik-Blacker.

My sisters, Joan and Cindy, and my brother, Murph, I'm grateful for their love and support. My dad, Sam, my thanks is equaled by the wish that I knew him better.

To our family cat of 21 years, Ajax, I'll keep stretching just the way you did.

Finally, to my mom, she's gravity and oxygen for so many. She's my best friend. My gratitude to her is too vast to contemplate.

I'll round the refund up to five cents. That's as high as I can go.